Here is the long-awaited companion volume to the international best-seller *The Master Plan of Evangelism*. In *The Master Plan of Discipleship*, Dr. Robert Coleman examines the Book of Acts to reveal how the early Church carried out Christ's command to "make disciples of all nations." Through this study, he shows us the pattern for disciple making. A book for *all* Christians, *The Master Plan of Discipleship* will help you and your church be more effective in carrying out the Great Commission today.

"I am grateful that Robert Coleman has shared his wealth of experience as a disciple maker with the Church at large. This book is the kind of tool we are constantly searching for in our church."

Frank R. Tillapauch, Pastor
Bear Valley Baptist Church
Denver, Colorado

"Dr. Coleman's insights on the ministry of discipleship are both profoundly biblical and wonderfully practical."

Paul Cedar, Pastor
Lake Avenue Congregational Church
Pasadena, California

"Dr. Robert Coleman, one of the most important voices for evangelism in America, has pointed the way to reach past the cynicism of modern secular man. The church has the message and the means to effect this change. Dr. Coleman has given us the method."

Jess Moody, Pastor
First Baptist Church of Van Nuys, California

D0378068

BY **Robert E. Coleman:**

Established by the Word
Introducing the Prayer Cell
Life in the Living Word
The Master Plan of Evangelism
The Spirit and the Word
Dry Bones Can Live Again
One Divine Moment (Editor)
Written in Blood
Evangelism in Perspective
They Meet the Master
The Mind of the Master
Songs of Heaven
Growing in the Word
The New Covenant
The Heartbeat of Evangelism
Evangelism on the Cutting Edge (Editor)
The Master Plan of Discipleship

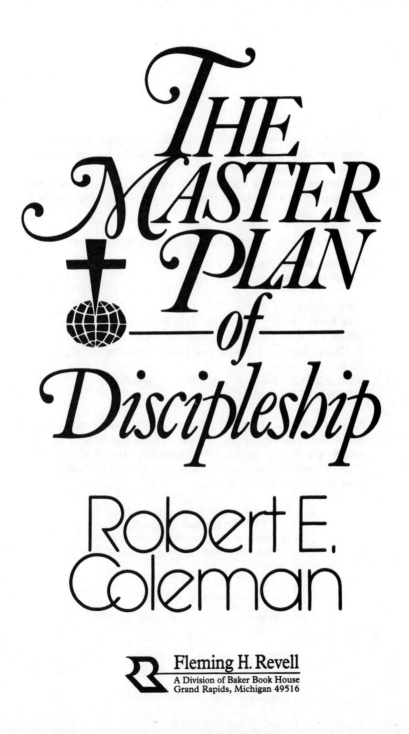

THE MASTER PLAN of Discipleship

Robert E. Coleman

Fleming H. Revell
A Division of Baker Book House
Grand Rapids, Michigan 49516

Unless otherwise identified, Scripture quotations are from the American Standard Version, copyrighted 1901 by the International Council of Religious Education.

Scripture quotations identified AMP are from the Amplified New Testament © The Lockman Foundation 1954–1958, and are used by permission.

Library of Congress Cataloging-in-Publication Data

Coleman, Robert Emerson, 1928–
  The master plan of discipleship.

  Bibliography: p.
  1. Bible. N.T. Acts—Criticism, interpretation,
etc. 2. Christian life—Early church, ca. 30–600.
3. Church history—Primitive and early church, ca.
30–600.   I. Title.
BS2625.2.C63   1987   226'.606   86-26043
0-8007-5237-6 (paper)

Copyright © 1987 by Robert E. Coleman
Published by Fleming H. Revell
a division of Baker Book House Company
P.O. Box 6287, Grand Rapids, MI 49516-6287

ISBN: 0-8007-5237-6

Seventh printing, April 1994

Printed in the United States of America

TO the Lausanne Committee for World
Evangelization,
colleagues in the bonds of the Great Commission,
who share the vision of the completed mission
of the coming King

Contents

Introduction

The Great Commission

Discipling men and women is the priority around which our lives should be oriented.

Why do we say this? because Jesus Christ Himself said it in His final words before His Ascension into heaven.

Matthew's account sums it up: "Go ye therefore, and make disciples of all the nations, baptizing them into the name of the Father and of the Son and of the Holy Spirit: teaching them to observe all things whatsoever I commanded you . . ." (Matt. 28:19, 20).[1] Significantly, in the original text, "go," "baptizing," and "teaching" are parti-

---

1. All undesignated Scripture references are from the Book of Acts and, unless otherwise specified, are taken from the American Standard Version of 1901.

ciples. This means that these responsibilities derive their
direction from the leading verb, "make disciples," or as
it might be translated, "make learners" of Christ.[2]

It shouldn't seem strange that the Master Teacher places
such a high priority on discipling. After all, Jesus was
simply asking His followers to do what He had done with
them. That is why they could understand it. As they had
freely received, now they were to transmit what they had
learned to other seekers of truth. The mandate was the ar-
ticulation of the rule by which Christ had directed His
ministry. Though slow, and not accomplished without
great sacrifice, He knew His way would succeed. For as
individuals learn of Him and follow the pattern of His life
they will invariably become disciplers, and as their disciples in turn do the same, someday through multiplication
the world will come to know Him whom to know aright
is life everlasting.

A Ministry Life-style

The Great Commission is not a special calling or a gift
of the Spirit; it is a command—an obligation incumbent
upon the whole community of faith. There are no exceptions. Bank presidents and automobile mechanics, physi-
cians and schoolteachers, theologians and homemakers—
everyone who believes on Christ has a part in His work
(John 14:12).

---

2. The word *disciple* designates a learner or follower, as in the
sense of an apprentice, and "always implies the existence of a personal attachment which shapes the whole of life of the one described."
Gerhard Kittel, ed., *Theological Dictionary of the New Testament,*
trans. and ed. Geoffrey W. Bromiley, vol. 4 (Grand Rapids, Mich.: Wm.
B. Eerdmans, 1967), 441.

Biblically speaking, we cannot define *clergy* and *laity* as mutually exclusive terms. In the bonds of Christ, all are laity (or the people of God) and equally share the responsibility to make disciples. By the same criteria, the whole body of believers receive the inheritance of Christ, which is the root idea of the term in the New Testament from which *clergy* is derived.[3] Radical distinctions between the pulpit and the pew did not develop until well into the second century.

Professionalizing of clergy roles has tended to confuse responsibility for ministry on the part of the unordained. The effect has been to discount, if not nullify, the conviction that all believers are priests. Unfortunately, many Christians feel quite satisfied with the situation, content to allow paid clergymen and staff to do all the work. But even those who are more sensitive to their calling and want to be involved

---

3. The word is *kleros* ($\kappa\lambda\tilde{\eta}\rho\sigma\varsigma$). This noun form has the meaning of "a share, a land received by lot, or inheritance." The verb, *kleronomeo*, ($\kappa\lambda\eta\rho\sigma\nu\sigma\mu\epsilon\omega$) refers to the activity of dividing by lot or obtaining an inheritance. A related term indicates "the one receiving the allotment" or "heir." In the Old Testament the word may be used to determine God's will by casting lots, a reference also seen in the New Testament when the soldiers cast lots for the garment of Jesus (Matt. 27:35; Mark 15:24; Luke 23:34), and the lots used by the disciples to select a replacement for the traitor (1:17, 25, 26). When the reference is to recipients of God's promise as the church, the terms relate to all believers who have received the inheritance of Christ (8:21; 20:32; 26:18; Rom. 4:13, 14; 8:16; Gal. 3:18, 29; 4:1, 7; Eph. 1:11; Col. 1:12; 3:24; Titus 3:7; Heb. 6:17; 9:15; 11:7, 8; James 2:5; 1 Pet. 1:4; 5:3). In the New Testament usage of these terms, then, everyone in the church is a clergyman or an heir of God. A good treatment of this word group may be found in Colin Brown, *The New International Dictionary of New Testament Theology*, vol. 2 (Grand Rapids, Mich.: Regency Reference Lib., Zondervan, 1976), 295–303.

may experience a sense of frustration as they try to find their place of service. "After all," they may ask, "if I'm not a preacher or missionary or something of the kind, how can I be properly engaged in ministry?"

The answer lies in their seeing the Great Commission as a life-style encompassing the total resources of every child of God. Here the ministry of Christ comes alive in the day-by-day activity of discipling. Whether we have a "secular" job or an ecclesiastical position, a Christ-like commitment to bring the nations into the eternal Kingdom should be a part of it.

Acts of Apostles

How ministry becomes life-style is nowhere better portrayed than in the Acts of the Apostles. With keen sensitivity to spiritual reality and careful recording of historical fact, the book describes the way Christ's command unfolds in the lives of His disciples. Special attention focuses upon great leaders, notably Peter and Paul, but the underlying story concerns the church, the ongoing body of Christ in the world. As such, it constitutes the second volume of the Gospel of Luke, "the former treatise" being the account of what Jesus "began both to do and to teach," while Acts depicts what He continues to do through the multiplying ministry of His disciples (Acts 1:1; cf. Luke 1:1-4).[4] By its nature, then, the mission that

---

4. Though not specified in Acts, Luke the physician, a cultured, well-educated Greek, is generally recognized by church tradition and scholarship as the author of the book. By his Gentile background, medical training, keen observations of human nature, and close association with the missionaries, he would be eminently qualified to write the account. Some even speculate that Luke was a con-

Christ initiated alone becomes in Acts a corporate movement. His objective and ministry are the same, only now
they are diffused through all His people. Validating the
witness, Christ's Spirit indwelling the church shines
through every page.

Much could not be recorded, of course. Great historical
writings, like masterpieces of art, must omit a great deal
in order to concentrate attention upon the most critical
points. Accordingly, the author singles out some leading
persons and decisive movements, lifting out a few characteristic scenes for elaboration and passing over the rest
with scarcely a mention. In this manner he creates a vivid
feeling for the whole, while always keeping before the
reader the main theme of the composition.

That controlling purpose is to document the powerful
beginnings of Christianity, showing how the Spirit of
Christ flows through His church, against which the gates
of hell cannot prevail. The narrative describes *acts,* not
committee meetings or study conferences. Miracles are
happening; lives are being transformed; the world is
being turned upside down. In the space of one generation,
a little company of Jesus' disciples with explosive force
sweeps from Jerusalem to Rome and develops from a
small sect into a universal church. Nothing can defeat
them—not the beatings of swaggering tyrants, not the
cunning of embittered religious rulers, not the internal
struggles of discontented members—but like a mighty army

---

vert of Paul, being the doctor summoned to care for the apostle at
Troas, at which time he heard the Gospel and was saved. Indeed, he
might have been the man through whom the Macedonian call came
(Acts 16:6–10). It is a fact that at this point in the narrative the word
"we" begins to appear and most of what follows appears to be re-
ported firsthand.

with banners, they move out to disciple the nations in the Name of their risen and reigning Lord.

Purpose of the Book

Years ago I sought to trace the underlying strategy of Jesus' personal ministry in my book *The Master Plan of Evangelism.*[5] That study in the four Gospels deducted some basic principles of discipling by observing how our Lord ordered His life, my conviction being that His way established guidelines for His disciples to follow.

This present study purposes to discern how the apostolic church carried out His mandate. Primarily using the Acts as reference, my design has been to see an unfolding pattern, especially noting principles of Christ's example in their witness. When these general concepts are before us, we have some landmarks by which to chart our present course.

I recognize that the way the first generation of Christians confronted their world does not fix specific policies for the twentieth century. Truth always must be seen in the context of the time and place where people live. It is well to remember, too, that the early church was still in a formative period, without well-defined precedents outside the Judaistic tradition. Things were still comparatively simple and rather flexible. Yet while structures and methodologies may change, principles remain constant in every age and culture. If we can see these foundational

---

5. First published in 1963, the book has gone through many printings and has been translated in numerous languages. It is available from Fleming H. Revell Company, Old Tappan, New Jersey.

truths in embryonic form, despite nineteen hundred years of cultural change, some basic guidelines can be established for the contemporary church. In fact, since movements tend to drift from their moorings with the passing of years, it is imperative that religious traditions and institutions continually be measured by the original pattern.

Study Plan

In my quest to discover these enduring principles, I have read the Acts of the Apostles many times and from many angles, comparing it with other New Testament accounts of the church and often perusing the Greek text. My desire has been to let the Scripture speak for itself, because I believe the Bible is its own best interpreter. In special areas of interest in which further elucidation was desired, I have consulted reference works in the field. Some of these supplementary sources will be cited in the footnotes.[6]

While mindful of the principles of Christ's ministry discussed in my earlier work on His life, I have not felt con-

6. A general bibliography on Acts is compiled by Richard N. Longenecker, *The Acts of the Apostles,* The Expositor's Bible Commentary, gen. ed., Frank E. Galbelein, vol. 9 (Grand Rapids, Mich.: Zondervan, 1981), 240–243. For a complete listing of commentaries, monographs, and articles up to the mid-sixties, *see* A. J. and M. B. Mattill, *A Classified Bibliography of Literature on the Acts of the Apostles* (Leiden: Brill, 1966). If one is interested in the way the book has been handled by scholars in New Testament criticism, a competent survey is by W. Ward Gasque, *A History of the Criticism of the Acts of the Apostles* (Tubingen: J. C. B. Mohr, 1975). An excellent selected bibliography of works on the early church, arranged according to topics, will be found in Everett F. Harrison, *The Apostolic Church* (Grand Rapids: Wm. B. Eerdmans, 1985), 237–251.

strained to use the same terminology or outline in this study. We are dealing now with a longer period of history and many more people, so this book unfolds around chapter themes appropriate to that larger context. No order of priority is implied in the sequence, since all the concepts are interrelated and should be seen together.

The book begins with our Lord's vision of the Kingdom and the coming of His universal reign through reproduction of disciples. In an attempt to deal with the problem of the aimless and self-serving multitudes, attention then turns to the need for concentrating effort upon persons wanting to learn of Christ and upon those who will labor in His harvest, underscoring the principle of selection. The training ground for this growing force of learners is seen in the close association of believers and their care for one another. This school of life demonstrates the power of the Gospel. As the church mobilizes for ministry to the world, leaders come forth and work in the responsibilities delegated to them. Faith becomes active through consecration, bringing discipline and supervision into the movement. The enabling power of the Holy Spirit, imparting the life of Christ in and through the church, concludes the review.

Though I have primarily focused on inductive biblical study, I have also attempted to suggest practical implications of the truth to our situation.[7] How can we be the church of the Great Commission today? My conviction is that if making disciples of all nations is not the heartbeat

---

7. A study of Acts with a somewhat similar purpose, but following more of a devotional format, is by Leroy Eims, *Disciples in Action* (Wheaton, Ill.: Victor Books, 1981). This book lifts out many practical applications of the narrative regarding discipleship.

of our life, something is wrong, either with our under-standing of Christ's church or our willingness to walk in His Way.

A Personal Yearning

At the outset let me state that I do not have all the an-swers. At best I only see through the glass darkly, as doubtless some of my readers will heartily agree. Many questions remain unresolved in my mind. But I believe that in His Word God has given us sufficient revelation to move forward. The Bible makes no mistakes. What I fail to understand in its inerrant message does not concern me nearly as much as what I do understand.

The more I have probed the dynamic of those first-century disciples, the more I am made aware of my own impotency. It is like comparing a river at flood stage with a trickling creek. The contrast leaves me convicted. J. B. Phillips, introducing his translation of Acts, expressed the feeling when he said "to turn from the vitality of these pages to almost any other current Christian writing, be it a theological book or a church periodical, is to bring tears to Christian eyes."[8]

Yet how invigorating is the change of outlook! Getting into the Book of Acts is like opening a window in a stuffy room. The wind of the Spirit blows through it. Here is re-ality. Feeling its emerging freshness, we should neither try to excuse our spiritual ineptness, nor relegate its vital-ity to a bygone era. The apostolic church, not the prevail-

---

8. J. B. Phillips, *The Young Church in Action* (London: Geoffrey Bles, 1955), viii.

ing mediocrity of our religious community, sets the norm. Where we perceive our shortcomings, in all honesty, we should seek to bring our lives into conformity with the New Testament standard.

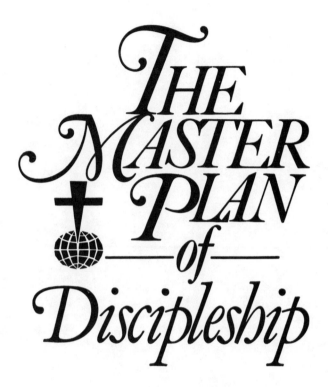

1

The Vision to Fulfill

An Upward Look

As the Book of Acts opens, Christ's disciples are looking upward, watching intently as the Lord ascends into heaven. Then ". . . a cloud received him out of their sight" (1:9).

In the Bible, a cloud often suggests an enveloping glory of the divine Presence. At the time of Moses a cloud hovered over the Tabernacle, signifying God's presence, and during the ministry of Christ on earth, a cloud overshadowed Him on the Mount of Transfiguration.

The cloud also has a prophetic impact. When Jesus described His glorious return to His disciples, He told them that they would see the Son of Man coming in the clouds of heaven.

What a fitting way to begin the Acts of the Apostles.

As the men still looked up two white-clothed angels stood by them and said: ". . . This Jesus, who was received up from you into heaven, shall so come in like manner as ye beheld him going into heaven" (1:11). That announcement reaffirms the promise of the final triumph of the church at the end of the age, when the Kingdom of God shall come in all its glory and every knee shall bow before Christ and every tongue confess that He is Lord (cf. Phil. 2:10).

Successors to the apostles always lived with this upward look. The church militant can never be separated from her destiny in the plan of God. What we may view as failures or successes in the work are only sequences in the sovereign will of Him who has determined the end from the beginning (cf. 2:23; 4:28). The past and future are eternally present in His mind. To comprehend the scope of evangelism, then, we must focus on the fulfillment of the Great Commission, a reality already celebrated in heaven around the throne of God (Rev. 5:9; 7:9).

Here, in the councils of eternity, we get perspective on earth's priorities: The movement of history reaches its conclusion; the pieces of the puzzle fit together. At the feet of Jesus, permanence dispels the passing contingencies of time, and we know even as we are known. Though now we only see vaguely the outline of that Kingdom, we know that it is certain and that someday Jesus Christ shall reign, King of kings and Lord of lords (Rev. 11:15; 17:14; 19:6).

The Coming Kingdom

It should not seem strange, then, that Acts begins with Jesus "speaking the things concerning the kingdom of God" (1:3). This was in view when we were created in His image to glorify His Name and serve Him in the beauty of holiness (Ps. 86:9; Isa. 43:21; Rev. 4:11). What makes sin so loathsome is that it repudiates God's purpose, causing mankind to worship the creature rather than the Creator (Rom. 1:20–25). Though an infinitely holy God must judge any perversion of His will, ultimately separating it from His Presence, He still loves that which He has made and ever seeks the restoration of a fallen race (e.g. Isa. 45:22).

His purpose unfolds awesomely in the call of Abraham, through whom God will raise up a special people to show His glory to the nations (Gen. 12:1–3; 18:18; 22:18; 26:4; cf. Acts 3:25). Abraham obeyed, utterly committing himself to the will of God, prefiguring that quality of devotion that characterizes children of the Kingdom. The promise was never realized in the faltering experience of Israel; but God promised that it would be when Shiloh came, their Messiah, who would bring forth peace and truth. He would be a light to the Gentiles and gather a people to serve Him from the ends of the earth (Gen. 49:10; Isa. 49:6). Evil then would be destroyed, justice exalted, and that rule of splendor, foreshadowed in the throne of David, established. "Of the increase of his government and of peace there shall be no end" (Isa. 9:7).

This expectation would come to fruition with the triumphant coming of the King. For ". . . behold, there came with the clouds of heaven one like unto a son of man, and he came even to the ancient of days, and they brought him near before him. And there was given him dominion, and glory, and a kingdom, that all the peoples, nations, and languages should serve him: his dominion is an everlasting dominion, which shall not pass away, and his kingdom that which shall not be destroyed" (Dan. 7:13, 14; cf. Zech. 9:10). In this prophecy the bringing of the nations to the Son of Man is seen as a gift God bestows to Himself, the revelation of His glory in the consummation of all things.

The Gospel of His Reign

Jesus ministered in the joyous confidence of this promise. Every step He took on earth was in anticipation of that day; the sound of the hosts of heaven praising God about the throne was vibrant in His soul. But He also knew that before His everlasting dominion could be realized, the world must be reconciled to God through the sacrificial offering of the Messiah-Son. To accomplish this mission, the Servant of the Lord had so to identify with our fallen estate that He would bear our sorrows, carry our griefs, and finally die in our place. There was no other way. Only by accepting our judgment in His own body could the Lamb of God take away the sin of the world (Isa. 53:1–12).

It is easy to see why, after the Resurrection, Jesus took such care to teach His disciples the meaning of these things, showing them the prophecies of Scripture. These men were His chosen vessels through whom the world was to believe on Him (John 17:20, 21), and unless they understood the purpose of His cross, how could His work be accomplished through them? So beginning with the Law of Moses and going through the Psalms and the Prophets,[1] Jesus explained how it was necessary "that the Christ should suffer, and rise again from the dead the third day, and that repentance and remission of sins should be preached in his name unto all the nations, beginning from Jerusalem" (Luke 24:46, 47).

This was the Gospel of the Kingdom—the good news of salvation to all people, which was embodied in Emmanuel's own life and work. The message found expression in the way He healed the brokenhearted, proclaimed release to the captive, offered recovering of sight to the blind, and provided freedom for those in bondage; all these were confirmed in His conquest of death and hell. In Him the Kingdom was already present; and in the inward sense of deliverance, all who come to Him in true repentance and faith enter His Kingdom—through spiritual rebirth (Mark 1:14, 15; John 3:3, 5; Matt. 18:3).

Yet the Kingdom is future in its completion, awaiting the coming of the Lord from heaven. Not until He returns in the glory of the Father will righteousness finally triumph with the dawning of a new age. In that day the heirs of Christ will see Him as He is and in perpetual praise dwell with Him forever.[2]

---

1. By referring to the three parts of the Old Testament, Jesus was saying that He was the central theme of all Scripture.

2. In this summation, I follow much the same approach to the Kingdom Gospel as F. F. Bruce, *Commentary on the Book of Acts* (Grand Rapids, Mich.: Wm. B. Eerdmans, 1980), 33–36. C. H. Dodd in *The Apostolic Preaching and Its Developments* (London: Hodder & Stoughton, 1936) does not include the Second Advent of Christ as a part of the Kingdom message, consistent with his view of "realized"

Until then, disciples living under His authority form a society of "called-out ones," the church.[3] As custodians of the Kingdom, followers of Christ display to this world the character of that age to come. Though perfect attainment awaits the day when all evil is banished, still the order of heaven establishes the ethic of God's people now. Christ's love becomes the rule of conduct, out of which flows the compulsion to make known the Gospel of His Kingdom in all the earth.

Earthbound Misconceptions

The tragedy of Jesus' time, no less than our own, is that most people misunderstand this Gospel.[4] Even His own

---

eschatology. A brief treatment of this subject is in Robert H. Mounce, *The Essential Nature of New Testament Preaching* (Grand Rapids, Mich.: Wm. B. Eerdmans, 1960), especially pp. 52–87.

3. The term "church," used more than a hundred times in the New Testament, comes from *ekklesia* (ἐκκλησία) meaning "called out ones." The word usually refers to a local body of Christians, though occasionally it is used to designate the aggregate of believers everywhere. In no place is it identified with a building, unless understood in the sense of the household of God. In Acts 7:38 and Hebrews 2:12 the word refers to God's people in the Old Testament, and in Acts 19:32, 41 it is used to denote the group of irate tradesmen called by Demetrius in Ephesus. For a concise development of the word, *see* Robert L. Saucy, *The Church in God's Program* (Chicago: Moody Press, 1972), 11–18; and Richard S. Taylor, "Church," *Beacon Dictionary of Theology* (Kansas City: Beacon Hill, 1983), 112–115. An exhaustive study of the term will be found in the article of Karl Ludwig Schmidt, in Gerhard Kittel, ed., *Theological Dictionary of the New Testament*, trans. and ed. Geoffrey W. Bromiley, vol. 4 (Grand Rapids, Mich.: Wm. B. Eerdmans, 1967), 501–536.

4. To corroborate this observation, one has only to peruse the writings and pronouncements of many liberal churchmen who espouse various forms of liberation theology. Though the motif of the Kingdom is freely employed and there is an appropriate recognition

disciples, though told of the Spirit's coming, did not readily comprehend the immediate spiritual nature of the Kingdom (1:4, 5). "Lord, dost thou at this time restore the kingdom to Israel?" they asked (1:6; cf. Luke 24:21). Like their contemporaries, they were thinking of the Messianic age in material terms, when their oppressors would be overthrown by force of arms and the Jewish nation restored. Likely still lingering in their minds was an earlier expectation of a political theocracy, with themselves sitting at the right and left hand of the throne (Matt. 20:21; 19:28). In their self-centered disposition, perhaps, they had not grasped Jesus' teaching about Christ's reign within their hearts. Nor had they comprehended the unassuming manner in which it comes by personal transformation, savoring society with the aroma of heaven through the witness of His church.

Little wonder that Jesus found it necessary to talk to them more about His Kingdom reign. They needed to understand that in the present age "the kingdom of God is within you" (Luke 17:21; cf. 17:20). As Paul later expounded, "The kingdom of God is not eating and drinking, but righteousness and peace and joy in the Holy Spirit" (Rom. 14:17). Not that there is no interest in making the present physical world a better place to live, but

of the prophetic cry for justice, these proponents of social humanism largely ignore or minimize the compelling need for personal salvation and thereby distort the redeeming force of the Gospel. All too easily the atoning work of the crucified, resurrected, and reigning Lord is lost in their references to Kingdom transformation. An evangelical needs to be very discriminating in embracing contemporary Kingdom rhetoric. For helpful insights concerning this issue, *see* Emilio A. Nuñez, *Liberation Theology*, trans. Paul E. Sywulka (Chicago: Moody Press, 1985); and William D. Taylor, "The Cry for Justice and Liberation," *Evangelism on the Cutting Edge*, ed. Robert E. Coleman (Old Tappan, N.J.: Fleming H. Revell, 1986), 59–74.

the eternal dimensions of life are spiritual in nature and can never be satisfied by bread alone.

Is there not still an inclination among persons of good-will to think in terms of material comfort and success? Our values tend to be determined more by fleshly gratification than the New Jerusalem. Concerning change in society, we are so accustomed to human manipulation, if not legislative coercion, that the quiet exercise of spiritual power seems unreal. Even where there is reliance on this unseen strength of God, too often it issues more from fanciful imagination than true faith in Christ.

The Living Christ

To eliminate any possibility of confusion in the hearts of the disciples, Jesus links His teaching concerning the Kingdom with His resurrection from the dead. "... He also showed himself alive after his passion by many proofs, appearing unto them by the space of forty days" (1:3). With this comprehensive statement, Luke establishes the claims of Christ's triumph over the confining forces of this world. At different times and in various places many persons actually saw the Lord in His glorified body; some talked with Him; others broke bread with Him or ate a meal that He had prepared; some held His hands and feet and even examined the spear wound in His side.[5] It is the kind of firsthand, objective evidence

---

5. Though not enumerated in Acts, there are ten separate instances of these resurrection appearances prior to His Ascension recorded in other New Testament accounts: (1) Mary Magdalene in the garden on the first Easter morning (John 20:11–18; Mark 16:9); (2) other women returning from the tomb (Matt. 28:9, 10); (3) two disciples, including Cleopas, enroute to Emmaus (Mark 16:12, 13;

that would stand up in a court of law. Clearly Jesus wanted His disciples assured of His bodily resurrection. This is no mystical mirage, no illusion of wishful thinking; rather they are witnesses to a very literal, visible, historical reality.

The observed Ascension of Christ speaks with the same certainty. By this manifestation of His glory, Christ impressed upon the disciples the order of His eternal reign with the Father. His sacrificial ministry on earth was ended in triumph, and henceforth no longer bound by the limitations of space and time, He assumed His ministry at the right hand of God. There He reigns in undisputed power over heaven and earth, awaiting the day of His majestic return.

Apostolic Preaching

The apostolic message is understood in the context of this reality. What was declared by Peter at Pentecost re-

---

Luke 24:13–32); (4) Simon Peter (Luke 24:34; 1 Cor. 15:5); (5) the eleven disciples in Jerusalem, except Thomas, who was absent (Luke 24:36–43); (6) the disciples, including Thomas, a week later (John 20:26–31); (7) the disciples by the Sea of Galilee (John 21:1, 2); (8) the eleven on a mountain in Galilee (Mark 16:14–18; Matt. 28:16–20), including probably 500 other brethren (1 Cor. 15:6); (9) James (1 Cor. 15:7); and (10) the disciples on the Mount of Olives (1:3–11; Luke 24:44–53; Mark 16:19, 20). To these might be added the postascension appearances to Paul on the Damascus Road (1 Cor. 15:8); Stephen at his martyrdom (7:55, 56); and John on the Isle of Patmos (Rev. 1:9–18). Collaborating these appearances was the evidence of the empty tomb in Joseph's garden (2:29–31; Luke 24:5, 6); the declaration of the angels (Luke 24:4–7); the report of the Roman guards (Matt. 28:11–15); and the phenomena of the saints released from their graves after Christ's resurrection (Matt. 27:51–53).

verberates throughout the Acts: Jesus of Nazareth, a man approved by mighty works, whom lawless persons cruci-fied, God has raised up, and exalted at His right hand, to which the outpouring of the Holy Spirit bears witness. Therefore, let everyone know assuredly that Jesus is both Christ and Lord (2:22–36).[6]

With this assurance the disciples proclaimed that the age of fulfillment had arrived, "the times of restoration of all things" (3:21). This was "the hope of the promise made of God unto our fathers" (26:6, cf. 28:20). All that had been prophesied about the suffering, death, and tri-umph of the Servant-King was accomplished in Christ, the Savior of the world. The stone the builders rejected was made the cornerstone. "Neither is there any other name under heaven, that is given among men, wherein we must be saved" (4:12).

Accordingly, the people were summoned to repent and believe on Christ, that they may receive forgiveness of

---

6. Generally all the summaries and excerpts of sermons in Acts follow this pattern, of which there are fourteen recorded. Peter is the spokesman in five (2:14–42; 3:13–26; 4:8–12; 5:29–32; and 10:34–43); one is by Stephen (7:2–60); and the others by Paul (13:16–41; 14:15–18; 17:22–31; 20:17–35; 22:1–21; 24:10–21; 26:1–27; 28:17–28). The sermons are addressed to God fearers, usually Jews, except those at Lystra (14:15–18) and Athens (17:22–31). Understandably these two sermons to purely pagans do not stress the exaltation of Christ as the fulfillment of Old Testament Scripture, but rather ap-peal to that revelation of God in nature and providence which any perceptive person could recognize (cf. Rom. 1:20f; 3:25). The mes-sage to the Ephesian elders at Miletus is the only recorded sermon addressed specifically to Christians (20:17–35). The student who would like more information about the sermons might read Donald Fraser, *The Speeches of the Holy Apostles* (London: Hodder & Stoughton, 1884); F. F. Bruce, *Speeches in the Acts of the Apostles* (London: Tyndale Press, 1942); and Robert Worley, *Preaching and Teaching in the Early Church* (Philadelphia: Westminster, 1967).

sins and the inheritance of those belonging to Christ (e.g.
2:38; 3:19; 5:31; 10:43; 13:38, 39; 17:30; 26:18, 20). The
moral demand is clear. Everyone must yield to the will of
God clearly disclosed in "the Holy and Righteous One"
(3:14). "And it shall be, that whosoever shall call on the
name of the Lord shall be saved" (2:21).

At its center is the affirmation of the Lordship of
Christ.[7] He is "the Judge of the living and the dead"
(10:42), the "Lord of heaven and earth" (17:24). To heir-
lings of earthly power this Gospel was received with scorn
and ridicule; but to the contrite and brokenhearted, it was
indeed the "good tidings of peace" (10:36). For the sovereign Lord was destined to rule over all; the enemies of
God would be put under His feet (2:35). The Kingdom
had come and is coming! This was the resounding message of Peter and Stephen and Philip and Paul and all the
other Christian witnesses (2:30; 3:21; 7:55; 8:12; 14:22;
19:8; 20:25; 28:23). So as the Acts begins with Jesus ex-
pounding the Gospel of the Kingdom, it ends with His
apostle telling the same story, "preaching the kingdom of
God, and teaching the things concerning the Lord Jesus
Christ" (28:31).

The considerable attention given to the content of the
apostolic message throughout Acts—approximately a

---

7. Underscoring this emphasis, the word *Lord* is used approximately 110 times in the Acts. If other terms were also considered
which imply Lordship, such as Judge or Prince, the number of references to this position of power would be much more. C. F. D. Moule,
in a study of the Christology in the writings of Luke, believes that the
title *Lord* is given more of a transcendental meaning in Acts, taking
its significance in a demonstrated way through the Resurrection.
"The Christology of Acts," *Studies in Luke-Acts,* ed. Leander E.
Keck and J. Louis Martyn (Nashville, Tenn.: Abingdon Press, 1966),
161.

quarter of the book—underscores the tremendous importance placed upon sound doctrine in the church.[8] Though
at this period complete systematic creeds had not been
formulated, certainly there was no lack of basic theological teaching, nor was there any confusion respecting the
essential truth of the Gospel.[9] Clearly Luke wanted to
emphasize that what they lived was inseparable from
what they believed.

To All Nations

The message by its nature cannot be self-contained. If
Christ is Lord of all, then every created being must recognize His claims upon his or her own life. Thus it was
written that His glory must be declared among the nations (1 Chron. 16:24; Ps. 97:6; 99:3–5); His fame must be
known to the isles afar off (Isa. 66:19). What God accomplished through Israel's Messiah was for the benefit of the
world, looking to the day when Gentiles and Jews come
together at the great banquet in heaven and God "hath
swallowed up death for ever" (Isa. 25:6–8).[10]

---

8. Of the 1,007 verses in Acts, about 280 refer to portions of sermons or Gospel testimony. By comparison, no more than 90 verses
speak of miracles and signs, and even fewer relate to matters of
church administration.

9. It does appear that simple confessions of faith were being used
before the end of the century, as may be indicated from such pas-
sages as Rom. 10:9; Matt. 16:16; 20:31; and 1 Cor. 15:3, 4. Discussed
by Oscar Cullman, *The Earliest Christian Confessions* (London: Leit-
terworth Press, 1949). We should keep in mind that the writings of
the New Testament, which were being circulated from this time on-
ward, constituted a full composition of Christian doctrine.

10. References to the Lord reigning over the nations abound
through the Old Testament, for example, Ps. 2:6; 10:16; 24:7, 8, 10;

This universal dimension of the Gospel comes naturally into the witness of the church. Christ's disciples were dispatched at Pentecost "unto the uttermost part of the earth" (1:8). Immediately its extensiveness was illustrated when the 120 Spirit-filled believers declared the wonderful works of God to representatives from no less than fifteen different nations that were present in Jerusalem for the feast, symbolizing "every nation under heaven" (2:5). As explained by Peter from the prophecy of Joel, God had said that His Spirit would be poured out "upon all flesh" that everyone might have opportunity to be saved (2:17). The invitation was not just to the international visitors, but ". . . to all that are afar off, even as many as the Lord our God shall call unto him" (2:39). Indeed, the promise given to Abraham reached to "all the families of the earth" (3:25).

Despite the disciples' hesitancy in making the application to the non-Jewish community, persecution forced them to put feet to their faith. Philip goes to Samaria, where he preaches Christ and the Kingdom (8:26–39). Meanwhile Saul is converted and told by the Lord that he will bear God's Name before the great and small of the earth (9:15; 22:15). The reluctant big fisherman, too, finally gets the message, which eventuates in the salvation of a Roman centurion and his household (10:1–48). So important is this breakthrough to the Gentiles that the story is twice repeated with confirming testimony of God's direction (11:1–18; 15:1–29).

Soon the good news comes to Antioch, where it is em-

29:10; 44:4; 47:2, 7, 8; 48:2; 68:21–24; 72:11, 14; 74:12; 84:3; 89:18; 95:3; 98:6; 99:4; 145:11; 149:2; Isa. 6:1, 2; 49:6; Jer. 10:10; Dan. 4:25; Zeph. 3:15; Zech. 14:16; Mal. 1:14; and many others.

braced by Greek-speaking as well as Aramaic Jews
(11:19–21). From this integrated congregation Paul and
Barnabas are sent out to take the Gospel to the world.
When their witness is scorned by the Jews at Antioch of
Pisidia, they turn to the Gentiles, as the Lord commanded
(13:46, 47). This becomes the pattern in city after city as
the missionaries seek to lift up the Lord of heaven and
earth who "made of one every nation of men" (17:26),
and who "commandeth men that they should all everywhere repent" (17:30). As the epic closes with Paul in
Rome, he is still preaching the universal love of God for
the human race.[11]

Continual Growth

What is seen in this vision to reach the world has its
corollary in church growth. The frequent mention of nu-

---

11. Paul was by no means the only crusading missionary in the
first generation. Though apostles were slow in leaving Jerusalem, it
appears that they, too, became ambassadors of Christ to distant
places. Peter likely preached in Rome. John and Philip evangelized
across Asia Minor. If we can believe church tradition, Andrew and
Bartholomew went to the Black Sea area; Thaddeus preached in
Persia; Matthew and Matthias got to Ethiopia; James reached Egypt;
and Thomas is thought to have traveled as far as India. Legend has it
that Mark, the Gospel writer, founded the church in Alexandria. We
dare not overlook, also, the thousands of nameless Christians who
faithfully bore their witness for Christ as they went about their business across the civilized world. A limited statement on the travels of
the apostles may be found in Edgar J. Goodspeed, *The Twelve* (New
York: Holt, Rinehart & Winston, 1957), 94–100. The geographical
extension of the church before Constantine is traced concisely by
Kenneth Scott Latourette in *A History of the Expansion of Christianity,* vol. 1 (New York: Harper & Bros., 1937), 66–114. A more complete coverage is the two-volume work of Adolf Harnack, *The
Mission and Expansion of Christianity in the First Three Centuries,*
trans. and ed. James Moffatt (New York: Williams & Norgate, 1908).

merical expansion appears to be by design. The writer of
Acts wants us to realize that the apostolic witness had
measurable results.

So following the outpouring of Pentecost about three
thousand receive the good news and are baptized (2:41).
Moreover, every day thereafter "the Lord added" to the
church "those that were saved" (2:47). Soon the number
of men alone (as distinct from women and children) ap-
proximated five thousand (4:4). Outward threatenings by
the Jewish authority and fearful judgment upon two hypocrites within the church only seem to accelerate the
growth, as "believers were the more added to the Lord,
multitudes both of men and women" (5:14). By the sixth
chapter addition has changed to multiplication as "the
word of God increased; and the number of the disciples
multiplied in Jerusalem exceedingly ..." (6:7).[12] Even
"... a great company of the priests were obedient to the
faith," indicating that numbers of persons in this most re-
sistant group in Israel were at last coming to Christ
(6:7).[13]

---

12. C. H. Turner has observed that Acts may be divided into six
sections, each covering about five years and concluding with a brief
reference to growth of the church (6:7; 9:31; 12:24; 16:5; 19:20; 28:31).
"Chronology of the New Testament," *Dictionary of the Bible* (New
York: Scribner, 1905), 421ff.

13. This is the first specific reference to any priests becoming followers of Christ, though earlier Barnabas is said to have come from a
Levitical family (4:36), and Zacharias and Simeon, godly men
awaiting the consolation of Israel, in the birth narratives embrace the
Lord. The Jewish historian Josephus (*The Life Against Apion,* vol. 1
[Cambridge, Mass.: Harvard Univ. Press, 1926], 335) claims that
more than 20,000 priests served in the temple, so that "a great company" could have indicated a sizable group. Significantly, too, the
word translated "were obedient" is in the Greek imperfect tense, denoting repetition, that is, priests were continually becoming identified with the Christian community. This may explain why at this

More ruthless persecution serves to drive believers to nearby regions, and as they go they preach the Word (8:4). Typifying this dispersion was Philip's witness to the Samaritans, where many "gave heed" and were baptized (8:6, 12). The witness is further spread to villages by Peter and John (8:25). Then an Ethiopian is converted on the road to Gaza, after which Philip preaches the Gospel "through ... all the cities, till he came to Caesarea" (8:40). Saul of Tarsus, the Sanhedrin's chief prosecutor, on his way to arrest believers in Damascus, is transformed by Christ and begins boldly to proclaim his newfound Lord. "So the church throughout all Judaea and Galilee and Samaria had peace, being edified; and, walking in the fear of the Lord and in the comfort of the Holy Spirit, was multiplied" (9:31).[14]

Some harassed saints settled in Lydda, where Peter visits and heals a paralytic man. Scripture reports that "all that dwelt at Lydda and in Sharon saw him, and they turned to the Lord" (9:35). At Joppa many believed, following the raising of Tabitha (9:42). From there Peter goes to Caesarea to bring the Gospel to the Roman officer, and Cornelius and his house are saved (10:44–48; 11:14). Other disciples go to people still more removed from their Jewish roots, and at Antioch "a great number" of Gentiles turn to the Lord (11:21), an ingathering re-

point the Jewish rulers seem to be more determined to stamp out the church.

14. The word *edified* conveys the idea of building a house and is often used in reference to progress. Also, the term *walking* carries the sense of going ahead with resolute purpose and dedication. Certainly the church is moving out for God. The reference to multiplication applies not only to numbers but to growth in spiritual reality. C. E. Aufrey, *Evangelism in Acts* (Grand Rapids, Mich.: Zondervan, 1964), 16, 17.

peated when Barnabas visits the church (11:24, 26). Though Herod singled out some of the Christian leaders for persecution, killing James and imprisoning Peter, still "the word of God grew and multiplied" (12:24).

With the sending of Paul and Barnabas by the church at Antioch, growth increasingly follows a global course. Moving into Asia Minor, wherever the witness is heard, persons turn to Christ (13:12, 42; 14:21). At Antioch of Pisidia "... almost the whole city was gathered together to hear the word of God" (13:44), and despite hostility, "as many as were ordained to eternal life believed. And the word of the Lord was spread abroad throughout all the region" (13:48, 49). It is much the same story at Iconium, Lystra and Derbe (14:1, 20, 21, 27), where Christians "were strengthened in the faith, and increased in number daily" (16:5). Challenged by the Macedonian vision, the missionaries travel into Europe—to Philippi, Thessalonica, Berea, Athens, Corinth, and neighboring regions, reaping a harvest of souls (16:15, 33, 34; 17:4, 12, 34; 18:8). Back and forth they move across the Mediterranean world, making disciples who in turn disciple others, until it is said that "all they that dwelt in Asia heard" the Gospel (19:10; cf. 26; 24:5). Even their enemies admitted that the Christians "turned the world upside down" (17:6). Truly the Word of the Lord grew "mightily" and "prevailed" (19:20).[15]

---

15. The word "mightily" *kratos* (κράτος), from Homer onwards, denotes power, strength, rule or victory. It may also be used as an attribute and title of kings, including deity (1 Pet. 5:11; Rev. 1:6; 5:13). Here it describes God's power at work among men through the Gospel witness. The term "prevailed," *ischuo* (ἰσχύω), carries a similar meaning, emphasizing the superior power of one in contrast to the impotence of others, as in the work of Christ (Mark 5:4; Luke 8:43; 14:6, 29; 20:26). This superiority is evident in the spread of the Word

Acts closes with the witness firmly planted in the capital of the world, the message of Christ going forth "with all boldness" (28:31). There is no conclusion. Indeed, there can be none, for we are still living in that age of the harvest, and it will continue until the work is finished. Yet in the space of little more than thirty years the witness had reached "the uttermost part of the earth" as Jesus had commanded (1:8). Paul could speak of the Christian faith as being proclaimed "throughout the whole world" (Rom. 1:8; cf. Col. 1:5, 6). In the general sense of making known the Gospel to all nations, certainly the apostolic church took the Great Commission seriously, and to a remarkable degree, actually succeeded in penetrating vast segments of the habitable world with the claims of the Kingdom.[16]

---

of God. Significantly, it is the same word Jesus used when He said that "the gates of Hades shall not prevail" against His church (Matt. 16:18). It would seem that Luke is relating the surging movement of Acts to the fulfillment of Christ's prophecy. For more word study, check with Colin Brown, *The New International Dictionary of New Testament Theology,* vol. 3 (Grand Rapids, Mich.: Regency Reference Lib., Zondervan 1976), 712–714, 716–718.

16. Kenneth Scott Latourette observes that "never in the history of the race has this record ever quite been equalled." Other movements in their inception, like Islam and Communism, may have gained more adherents in the same length of time, but that was chiefly by force of arms. But no "religious faith, or, for that matter, any other sect of ideas, religious, political or economic, without the aid of physical force or cultural prestige, achieved so commanding portion" in so short a time as Christianity. *History of the Expansion of Christianity,* 112.

Principle of Multiplication

Considering that the church prior to Pentecost numbered only a few hundred believers, this is an astounding achievement.[17] Probably the Christian community within three decades had multiplied four hundredfold,[18] which represents an annual increase of 22 percent for more than a generation, and the rate of growth continued remarkably high for 300 years. By the beginning of the fourth century, when Constantine was converted to Christianity,

---

17. The exact numerical strength of the church at this period cannot be determined, but it would certainly reach into multiplied thousands. There were myriad believers among the Jews alone (21:20), and with the Gentiles added to this, there may well have been upwards of 200,000 Christians. By the end of the century, the total strength of the church has been estimated at .5 million among the 100 million inhabitants of the Roman Empire, though this figure may be excessive. See Philip Schaff, *History of the Christian Church*, vol. 1 (Grand Rapids, Mich.: Wm. B. Eerdmans, 1950), 196. Supporting a large number is the report, quoted by Adolf Harnock, that Nero, Paul's contemporary, noticed that not only at Rome, but everywhere multitudes were daily falling away from idolatry and embracing the new religion (*Mission and Expansion* 2:16). The Roman historian Tacitus' mention of "immense multitudes" martyred by Nero also suggests a large Christian population (Schaff, *History of the Church* 1:196). Justin Martyr, writing in the second century, said that Christians were spread "throughout the cities of the world." Indeed, he observed, "there is not a single race of human beings, barbarians, Greeks ... nomads or vagrants or herdsmen ... where prayers in the name of Jesus the crucified are not offered up" (Harnock, *Mission and Expansion* 2:4, 5). Tertullian, eminent church father of the same period, similarly spoke of the Christians filling "every corner of the universe," with the result that "the whole ends and bounds of the world are occupied with the Gospel" (ibid., 7, 16). Clemons Romanus and Ignatius expressed the same convictions (ibid., 24).

18. This is computed on the basis of 500 believers before Pentecost (1 Cor. 15:6), estimating the church strength at close to 200,000 at the close of the Acts era.

the number of disciples may have reached 10 or 12 million, or roughly a tenth of the total population of the Roman Empire.[19]

Such growth cannot be sustained by merely adding the children of Christians to the rolls, nor is it the result of large transfers of membership from other congregations. The early church grew by evangelistic multiplication as witnesses of Christ reproduced their life-style in the lives of those about them.

It does not matter how small the group is at the beginning, provided that they implant their vision in men and women who will in turn pass the word along to others and that they also reproduce. The early church gave eloquent witness to the dynamic in the hearts of people who take God at His Word and believe that with Him nothing is impossible.

Application Today

Times change, of course. Nothing in our society is ever stationary. But the command to reach the world for Christ remains the same. The Book of Acts makes clear that bringing the Gospel to every creature is God's program, and it can be accomplished.

World evangelization, considered in its full spiritual dimension, complements vital Christianity. Indeed, it is part of the Kingdom vision. Here is a divinely ordered goal for every Christian. Not only is it attainable; it is inevitable. Whether or not we believe it, someday the Gospel of the Kingdom will be heard to the ends of the earth

---

19. Schaff, *History of the Church* 1:197. Some estimates are higher.

(Matt. 24:14). The God of the universe will not be defeated in His purpose. Any activity not in step with His design for human destiny is an exercise in futility. The sooner we realize this and align our way with His, the sooner we will be relevant to eternity.

How critically the church needs the Kingdom vision—a vision born of the Word of God and the reality of His will for humankind. Too easily we have settled for less, letting the world set our agenda, while the priorities of heaven are ignored. All the while the aimless multitudes drift ever nearer to destruction, without a song to sing or a cause to espouse.

In this light, is it not appropriate to ask ourselves, "What is God's aspiration for our lives?" Only after we have determined where our Lord wants us to go can we make plans to get there.

The issue turns on our view of God and His Gospel to the world. If we are assured that the King of Glory, having taken our sins away and shattered death in conquest of the grave, will save unto the uttermost all that come to Him, then we cannot sit idly by while men and women perish without hope. We dare not show unconcern for the world God loves and for which He gave His beloved. The good news of salvation must be heralded to the ends of the earth. Jesus is Lord! He reigns on high and is coming again in majesty and power. Just the thought makes the heart almost miss a beat in wonder! We may not amount to much, but we have a great Savior, and His Kingdom is forever.

Here is where we begin. How this vision will be realized, however, brings us to consideration of another principle in the unfolding drama of redemption.

2

The People to Win

Earth's Misfits

Apostolic Christians had no illusions about the task at hand. They knew that the rulers of the earth "were gathered together, Against the Lord, and against his Anointed" (4:26; cf. 13:27). Everywhere there were "despisers" of Christ (13:41), persons "filled with jealousy" and hatred (13:45), who scorned the things of God. It was indeed a "crooked generation," insatiated with perversion and immorality (2:40), and "evil affected against the brethren" (14:2).

In such a society, not surprisingly, the church was hard pressed. The Romans, though generally tolerant of religious beliefs, looked upon the Christians as a deviant, antisocial cult.[1] Persons who confessed Jesus as Lord would not bow down to pagan gods or take part in the customary imperial worship, which caused them to be commonly branded as athiestic and unpatriotic. Strangely, too, the loving relationships developed among the Christians, together with their secret observance of the Eucharist, led the rabble to charge them with lust and even cannibalism. We may wonder how such slanderous accusations could be sustained, but then misguided persons who feel threatened seldom bother to look for facts to correct embittered notions. Making the Christian life-style even more challenging was their austere ethic of purity, which stood in judgment upon the immorality of their day. Believers, for example, would not attend the popular gladiatorial games, or take part in the trade-guild feasts, which included the practice of temple prostitution. Such puritans easily were misfits in the sensate culture about them.

What invoked more consternation was the message proclaimed by the disciples. They claimed that a man crucified as a convicted criminal was none other than the eternal God, Creator and Ruler of the universe. Could

---

1. The Jews, who shared this same accusation, enjoyed an official recognition by the state, which put them in a different class from the Christians. As long as the disciples were considered part of the Jewish religion, they enjoyed something of this exception from Roman practice. But when the church became largely Gentile in its makeup, their situation became more precarious. For a resumé of the first-century conditions under which the church labored, *see* Michael Green, *Evangelism in the Early Church* (Grand Rapids, Mich.: Wm. B. Eerdmans, 1970), 29–47. A more complete discussion is by Robert Grant, *Early Christianity and Society* (New York: Harper & Row, 1977); and Wayne A. Meeks, *The First Urban Christians: The Social World of the Apostle Paul* (New Haven, Conn.: Yale Univ. Press, 1983).

anything be more preposterous? Having died for the
world, they claimed that He came from the dead and
ascended to reign at the throne of heaven, from which He
will return to judge the nations. As if this was not enough,
these followers of the lowly Nazarene dared to call upright citizens to repentance and faith in their Lord, a
mandate that they said must be applied to every class of
people on earth. To the idealistic Greeks, no less than the
power-oriented Romans, this message seemed utterly ri-
diculous. How could learned and sophisticated worldlings
show anything but disdain for the Gospel?

Jewish Opposition

Yet incompatible as the Christian faith and practice
were to the pagan world, it was not the secular authorities
who mounted the greatest opposition to the church.
There are only six instances of Roman hostility toward
the Christians recorded in Acts. Of these, half were the
result of initial Gentile bitterness (16:19–48; 19:23–41;
17:13; cf. 12:1–23; 14:2–6; 14:19), not counting the events
that led to the arrest and trial of Paul (20:3; 21:27–36;
22:22–30; 23:1–4ff; 23:12ff; 24:1–9; 25:1–7, 13–22; 25:23–
26:2ff). Later, persecution became more common from
the Romans,[2] but in the first years the Jewish religious
establishment precipitated most of the antagonism (2:13;
4:13–23; 5:17–33ff; 6:9–7:1, 54, 57ff; 8:1–3; 9:1, 2, 29; 13:8,

---

2. The first great official persecution came under Nero, about A.D.
64, though it appears to have been localized in Rome. Again toward
the end of Domitian's rule, at the close of the century, there was
widespread violence against Christians. Intermittent periods of persecution continued until the fourth century. A description of these
attacks will be found in any standard church history.

45, 50; 14:2, 5, 19; 17:5, 13; 18:5, 6, 12–17; 19:8–19). Altogether there are twenty-two separate accounts of some form of overt Jewish hostility toward Christians, which is nearly four times that ascribed to Gentiles.

One might have thought that kindred monotheists of a common race and tradition would welcome the Christian witness. After all, they shared the same Scriptures, observed the moral law, followed many of the same customs of worship, even had much the same zeal for the conversion of outsiders to their ways.[3] Certainly these similarities facilitated communication, making the full impact of the Gospel more understandable, a fact that the disciples recognized in their first efforts at evangelization. But it did not make the offense of the cross any less real. That God would become incarnate in Jesus appeared to be a contradiction of their concept of deity. How could the Almighty be divided? Also that their Messiah would take the form of a servant, finally to die on the stake, as one under a curse, to them seemed absurd.[4] Such preaching was a "stumbling block" to persons who believed salvation came through rigid conformity to the law.

---

3. Extensive Jewish proselytism, which flourished after the Maccabean period, was beginning to decline in this century, though it was still practiced, especially among the Pharisees. As Jesus observed, they would cross "sea and land to make one proselyte"(Matt. 23:15). The fervent Christian evangelism, though with a different thrust, in one sense was a continuation of this already established custom. Information about the Jewish practice may be found in Bernard J. Bamberger, *Proselytism in the Talmudic Period* (New York: Ktav Publishing House, 1968).

4. According to Deuteronomy 21:22, 23, any person hanged on a tree rested under a curse, which the Jews associated with crucifixion. It will be observed, however, that this "stake" was used by the apostles to powerful effect in their preaching (5:30; 10:39; 13:29; Gal. 3:13; 1 Pet. 2:24).

Adding to the provocation, Christians not only built no temple in which to worship, but they disregarded many of the sacred precepts of the ceremonial law, like circumcision and eating certain foods. How dare these renegade disciples of an unordained Carpenter-Teacher, without any formal seminary training, seek to undermine the age-long beliefs of God's chosen people? Sheer presumption! Those who were most astute fully realized that if the Gospel of grace was allowed to spread through Judaism, their whole legalistic system of religion, as officially practiced, would crumble. Persons who clearly see the issues cannot be indifferent. Opposition to the Great Commission invariably is most pronounced among unbelieving religious authorities.[5]

Corrupt Leadership

This is evident all through the movement of the church in Acts. It was the priests, "the captain of the temple,"and other "rulers of the people," who laid hands on Peter and John as they preached in Jerusalem (4:1–3, 8, 15). The high priest and his cohorts, "filled with jealousy," again had the apostles arrested and put in prison in an attempt to stop their ministry (5:12–18). Observing the great wonders and signs of Stephen, ruling members of the synagogue connived to have him stoned (6:3–15), among them

5. Despite the antipathy of their leaders, the masses of Jews still generally regarded the Christians with respect, until they refused to support the revolt against Rome in A.D. 63–73. This led to the charge that Christians did not have the national interest at heart, and from this time on few Jews were converted to Christianity. Feelings of enmity developed between them, creating bitterness and discrimination, which, regrettably, resulted in Christians taking the role of persecutors of the Jews in the time of Constantine.

Saul, the chief prosecutor of the Sanhedrin (8:1). When later Saul was converted, the local Jewish authorities and the Nabatean ethnarch made a concerted effort to kill him (9:23; cf. 2 Cor. 11:32, 33). At Pisidian Antioch, when influential Jews saw the tremendous interest in Paul's message, rather than trying to help the people understand the Gospel, "they . . . contradicted the things which were spoken by Paul," an incident that caused the missionaries to turn to the Gentiles (13:44–46). The same group then "urged on the devout women of honorable estate, and the chief men of the city" to expel the messengers from their coasts (13:50). Similarly, opposition was engineered by prominent Jews at Iconium (14:2), Lystra (14:19), Thessalonica (17:13), and Jerusalem (21:27–31; 22:30).

This tactic is not confined to the Jewish leadership, of course. Gentile hucksters at Philippi reacted in an identical manner when a slave girl in their employment was delivered from a spirit of divination. Seeing that their nefarious gain was gone, they brought the missionaries before the magistrates, charging them with teaching customs that were not lawful for Romans (16:16–21). Thus aroused, "the multitude rose up together against them," causing a commotion which ended with the magistrates ordering Paul and Silas beaten, then thrown in jail (16:22–24).

Likewise, in Ephesus, it was Demetrius, the silversmith, along with other craftsmen who made their livelihood from the sale of silver shrines, who persuaded the crowd to attack the Christians (19:23–32). They astutely recognized that, if the people converted to Christ, their trade would be in jeopardy, though they carefully phrased their concern in an emotional veneration of the popular goddess Diana.

One cannot help but notice in these accounts that unbelieving persons of influence usually provoke others to do their devious work. It would appear that manipulators don't like to get their own hands dirty. What makes the situation so pathetic is the acquiescence of the multitudes. They seem to go along unquestioningly, like aimless sheep, content to follow their leaders.

The Lost Multitudes

At heart, however, the masses were good-hearted, lovable people, with genuine humanitarian instincts. Generally they seemed respectful to the disciples, and despite their mixed reaction to the Gospel, they showed curious interest in the apostolic ministry. The quiet, assured manner of the Christians intrigued them.

They were especially impressed by the miraculous acts of compassion flowing from the Christian witness, being filled with awe at what they saw (e.g. 3:9–12; 4:13; 9:7, 35, 42). Fair-minded people appreciate tangible expressions of concern, something that even skeptics cannot gainsay. For example, following the healing of the lame man at the temple gate, the priests were afraid to do more than threaten Peter and John, "for all men glorified God for that which was done" (4:21). On another occasion, after a great manifestation of healing that attracted multitudes from the cities around Jerusalem, the captain and officers sent to arrest the apostles "brought them, but without violence; for they feared the people, lest they should be stoned" (5:12–26). It would have been dangerous to put in chains those miracle workers whom the people "magnified" (5:13).

The experience underscores a common trait of human

nature. People are easily excited to noble behavior when their own physical interests are served. After all, who can object to alleviating pain and suffering, the more so when long-standing ills are cured. Unfortunately, circumstances influence their decisions more than truth. The people of Jerusalem could be overwhelmed by the apostles' miracles, but a little later, coaxed by their leaders, they stoned Stephen to death. One might presume that it was surely a different crowd that killed him, and that might be true. But still one would have to ask, "Where were all those supporters when the chips were down?"

Time and time again we are made aware of the superficiality of the masses. They will ascribe to Simon the power of God, being bewitched by his sorcery in Samaria (8:9–11), then later rejoice in the mighty work of Philip, when he comes preaching Christ (8:5–8, 12, 13). Little wonder that the apostles, when they heard of the Samaritans turning to the Lord, felt constrained to send them teachers to give the converts more instruction in the Word (8:14–17).

Or take the reaction of the crowd at Lystra. During the visit of Paul and Barnabas, after a cripple is healed, the people conclude that the gods have come down to them (14:8–13). All of them, including the local priest of Jupiter, were so carried away by what they saw that the missionaries "scarce restrained ... the multitudes from doing sacrifice unto them" (14:18). Yet the very next verse of the account tells how certain Jews came down from Antioch and Iconium, and "having persuaded the multitudes, they stoned Paul, and dragged him out of the city, supposing that he was dead" (14:19). Incredible! One moment they want to worship the missionaries, then on second thought they decide to kill them.

Look at the people of Ephesus, where "fear fell upon them all, and the name of the Lord Jesus was magnified," when they saw the miracles by the hands of Paul (19:11–18). Something of a revival broke out. Those who had been involved in the occult brought their magical books and burned them in the sight of all (19:19). But not long afterward, in this city, the multitudes, provoked by the greedy merchants, were suddenly "filled with wrath," and rioted against the missionaries (19:28). "The assembly was in confusion," most of the people not really understanding why "they were come together" (19:32). Still the baser instincts of the mob prevailed, and for two hours they shouted "Great is Diana of the Ephesians" (19:34). It was only after the town clerk intervened and "quieted the multitude" that order was restored (19:35–41).

One might wonder how the masses could be so fickle, so unsteady, that they moved whimsically, without knowing the issues. But it is a characteristic of human nature. People tend to react impulsively and do things on the spur of the moment. The barbarians at Malta, who, noticing the viper hanging on Paul's hand, thought that he was a murderer; but when he shook it off and did not die, they "changed their minds, and said that he was a god" (28:3–6).

Underlying this variableness is a protective instinct of accommodation. The reaction to King Herod's speech at Caesarea is a graphic illustration. This tyrant, who had killed James and had Peter imprisoned, on this occasion was making an oration to the crowd gathered at a festival in honor of Caesar. As he spoke, the people shouted, saying it was "the voice of a god, and not of a man" (12:22), a blasphemous adulation that, when accepted, invoked the fearful judgment of the Lord upon the king. Of course, the people did not mean what they said. Actually they hated Herod. But seeking to incur his favor, they found it politically expedient to please him. Worldlings will perpetrate almost any deceit to assure their self-preservation and prosperity.

Such an attitude is easily recognized in the affairs of this world. Is not our first concern to protect ourselves and those who support us? We want to play it safe. That which will enhance our material security and comfort receives support, even if it means the deprivation and repression of others. To be sure, we may also have an innate desire for fair play—that is, when it does not entail inconvenience on our part. No wonder that the multitudes are so easily exploited by persons in positions of authority. When it comes down to taking action, the multitudes will take the course of least resistance. This is the problem we face in evangelism and discipleship, and unless we deal with it realistically, we are irrelevant to the situation.

Spiritual Blindness

Not surprisingly, then, the masses, with their self-centered inclination, resisted the claims of Christ. The problem is brought out forcefully by Stephen in his defense before the high priest and council of Jews at Jerusalem (7:1–53). Going back through the history of Israel, from the time of the patriarchs to the prophets, he showed how God's messages had repeatedly been rejected. Their present hostility toward Christ was nothing more than a continuation of an agelong attitude of disobedience. "Ye stiffnecked and uncircumcised in heart and ears, ye do always resist the Holy Spirit," he said. "As your fathers did, so do ye" (7:51). There was one difference, however. Their fathers only killed the messengers who foretold the coming of the Righteous One; while, in the present case, they had become the actual "betrayers and murderers" of the Messiah (7:52).

It is not difficult to understand that "when they heard these things, they were cut to the heart, and they gnashed on him with their teeth" (7:54). Persons who consider themselves quite respectable and law abiding never like to be told of their rebellious nature. They "cried out" against the preacher; they "stopped their ears"; and finally, in self-righteous indignation, they killed him (7:57, 58). Just as with the perpetrators of Christ's crucifixion, those unwilling to accept the truth tried to vindicate their perverted ways by silencing the messenger of God.

The Gospel of the crucified "Prince of life; whom God raised from the dead," will always come as an offense to this world (3:14, 15). It jerks off the mask of our pretentious glory and makes us face the twisted nature of fleshly values. That the Son of God would give His life to save others and not save Himself utterly cuts across the grain of ego centeredness. The measure of Calvary love is too high; its demands too uncompromising. It is all right to talk about moral improvement, even social reformation, but to expect complete renunciation of sin in loving submission to the claims of Christ is more than proud earthlings can accept.

God's good news simply does not make sense to the unrepentant. As Paul reminded the Romans, referring to the words of Isaiah, "Hearing ye shall hear, and shall in no wise understand; And seeing ye shall see, and shall in no wise perceive: For this people's heart is waxed gross, And their ears are dull of hearing, And their eyes they have closed" (28:26, 27; cf. Isa. 6:9, 10; Rom. 11:8). Interestingly, Jesus referred to this same passage in characterizing the people's resistance to His teaching (Matt. 13:14, 15; Mark 4:12; Luke 8:10; John 12:39, 40). Such persons, of course, never find the truth, for they have no desire to walk in the light. Content with darkness, they remain under the deception of Satan.

Thanks be to God those who are broken and humble in spirit will come to the Savior. Christ has brought light into the world, both to the Jew and to the Gentile (26:18). Through the abundance of God's grace and the quickening power of His Spirit, persons of any race or station who with all their heart seek God will find the way "if haply they might feel after him" (17:27). Enabling this quest to be fulfilled, Christians are sent to announce the Kingdom, in order that the eyes of the contrite may be opened, and "that they may turn from darkness to light" (26:18).

Selection in Acts

Just as Jesus did, the expanding church seeks out persons on the stretch for God and concentrates energy upon their development. This principle of selection can be seen at the onset of the Acts, with Jesus meeting with the disciples for a final briefing before He returns to heaven. He does not appear to the unreached masses of humanity, all of whom He died to save; rather He concentrates attention upon those few faithful men and women who were soon going forth as His ambassadors to the world. They were the key to the fulfillment of His mission.

When the Holy Spirit filled them at Pentecost, the disciples took their witness to the streets of the city, where thousands of people were gathered for a great religious celebration. Not a bad place to start—where a host of spiritually sensitive Jews from at least fifteen different nations were gathered. It is remarkably similar to the way Jesus began His active ministry by attending the great revival of John the Baptist, where He drew out His first disciples (John 1:29–51). Here, in the environs of the holy temple, the church grew quickly and drove her stakes deep, even as she moved out through her native soil in Judea.

The next big harvest comes at Samaria, a place where Jesus had earlier laid a foundation by His witness (John 4:4–42). Is it also a coincidence that the Ethiopian official who is approached by Philip had just been reading the prophecies of Christ in Isaiah? When the Gospel finally penetrates the Roman world, it is with a devout centurion—a spiritually minded man already inclined toward the faith of Israel—where the breakthrough comes. Observe, too, that it was at Antioch, a place where many God-fearing Greeks were attending Jewish services,[6] that the emerging Christians found a congenial setting for planting a predominantly Gentile church.

This pattern of concentration upon receptive people continues in the missionary journeys of Paul. In each place visited, invariably he goes first to the synagogue to explain to persons of like religious background that Jesus is the Christ (13:5, 14, 42, 43; 14:1; 17:1, 2, 10, 17; 18:4, 7, 19, 26; 19:8; cf. 22:19). At Philippi, where there was no

6. F. F. Bruce, *Commentary on the Book of Acts* (Grand Rapids, Mich.: Wm. B. Eerdmans, 1980), 239.

synagogue, he began by a riverside where Jewish worshipers would come to pray (16:13, 14). This is not to imply that the Jewish reception was always friendly, for as the Gospel became clear, he would be asked to leave the synagogue and, not infrequently, would receive the brunt of their indignation. Nevertheless there were always some yearning hearts waiting for the hope of Israel, and upon hearing the message, they recognized Christ as the object of their quest. Only after this natural door of entry was closed did Paul turn to the Gentiles. Even then, it was usually Hellenists who had some prior contact with Jewish Scriptures who were first to believe (e.g. 13:46–48).

Surely it is no accident, too, that among the receptive, individuals of unusual influence often received particular attention in the unfolding narrative. Not to suggest that Christians were prominent members of society. For, in fact, they were essentially of the common class, including numbers of slaves. They would have to be considered another ragged aggregation by any sophisticated standard. But there were some exceptional leaders drawn from their ranks.

Look for Disciples

Whatever the apparent gifts and abilities of people, however, we must look for those who want to move for Christ. Life is too short to expend excessive time and energy upon apathetic people. We need to minister to their needs, of course. Let them know we care, and sow Gospel seed among them. Genuine compassion will not be without its effect, and someday the tide will turn. But converting the world to the Savior is not within our power. That is God's work. Our part is to move with His Spirit and respond to those whose hearts have been awakened by grace.

The place to begin is with those within the orbit of our life most disposed to learn of Jesus. Not that others are less loved, but that our first concern is with those who are seeking truth. Our objective is the evangelization of the world, to be sure. But before much can be done to effectively reach the multitudes, the laboring force in the harvest must be multiplied. Every disciple made for Christ contributes to this ever-expanding working force. At any point in our life, I am convinced a few such persons are within the influence of every Christian.

Application Today

Here is the opportunity we have every day for fulfilling the Great Commission. When we pray for God to raise up laborers, we can believe that He will answer. We must look for them. Likely they will be among those persons who feel comfortable with us, perhaps coming from the same background, with similar interests and traits. Affinities in personality and temperament may also be apparent. In some instances, however, there may be no natural ties, and we will have to create an environment of trust. Almost any barrier can be overcome as long as one has a teachable spirit.[7]

This places a special responsibility upon encouraging the spiritual inclinations of our families and friends, as well as those with whom we regularly meet. In a very real

---

7. Where there seems to be a desire to learn, yet because of our differences in personality or culture we cannot relate easily, let us try to channel the person to someone with whom there may be more affinity. We can rejoice that God has so created diversity among people that there is room for everyone to disciple.

sense, we should accept these natural relationships as providentially arranged by God.[8]

In terms of the church outreach, it behooves us to understand the spiritual aspirations of the community. Where do people sense their need of help, including the hunger of the soul for God? Groups that are found more open to the Gospel should receive priority attention. We must not only locate these people, but build bridges of understanding and love with them. The same pertains to the missionary thrust on a global scale.

Even in penetrating unreached peoples the principle applies.[9] Ministry to the larger community will disclose those sensitive to the message of Christ. These persons then can receive more cultivation and teaching, until they embrace the Gospel and become the evangelizers of their people group. Usually it is not the foreign missionary who wins the multitudes of a newly reached tribe. Rather the great harvest is reaped by those persons within the culture having natural identity with the people.

The strategy of evangelizing in any situation hinges

---

8. The Institute for American Church Growth asked over 14,000 people the question: "What or who was responsible for your coming to Christ and your church?" They report that 75–90 percent indicated that the primary human factor was the influence of a friend or relative. Cited by Win and Charles Arn, *The Master's Plan for Making Disciples* (Pasadena, Calif.: Church Growth Press, 1982), 43.

9. An unreached people is defined by some church growth specialists as a group that is less than 20 percent practicing Christian. Another way the category may be defined is by noting the presence or absence of a viable, reproducing church. Edward R. Dayton, "To Reach the Unreached," in *Perspectives on the World Christian Movement,* ed. Ralph D. Winter and Steven C. Hawthorne (Pasadena, Calif.: Wm. Carey Lib., 1981), 581–596. Incidentally, everyone interested in the biblical, historical, cultural and strategic dimensions of world evangelization should get into this multifaceted collection of readings from seventy leading authors.

upon men and women who will lead their followers to Christ. This places a premium upon reaching persons already with an evident following. However, if such persons are not within our present circle of influence, then let us begin where we are and develop the potential leadership of those few learners God has opened to our instruction. One does not have to be a superstar to impact the world for God. Anyone willing to follow Christ can become an effective leader of others.

But how do these budding disciplers learn the way of the Messiah? Where will they get proper training? To answer this question, we need to focus on another principle in the apostolic church.

3

The Fellowship to Cherish

Body Life

In the Book of Acts, those who responded to the Gospel invitation were brought immediately into association with other persons of like faith. This fellowship of kindred spirits constituted "the church of the Lord" (20:28), those called out from the world to follow Christ.

The community of disciples became the primary means by which disciples were trained. Just as Jesus had lived closely with His followers, so now the gathered community of believers formed an ongoing communion with His Spirit.

In a visible, present sense, the church filled the role of Christ's body in the world (1 Cor. 12:27).[1] Christ was the head (Eph. 1:22; Col. 1:18; 2:19), with the redeemed functioning as vital members of the body and thereby "severally members one of another" (Rom. 12:5; cf. 12:4; 1 Cor. 12:20). Not all the believers had the same office (Rom. 12:4), but "according to the grace that was given" (Rom. 12:6), all served in some useful way the work of the body (Eph. 4:11, 12). Within this ministering fellowship, as followers of their Lord, they helped one another grow and mature in "the measure of the stature of the fulness of Christ" (Eph. 4:13).

It was like a loving family. God was their Father (Rom. 4:11; Gal. 3:26), and as His sons and daughters (2 Cor. 6:18; Gal. 3:26), they shared equally the inheritance of Christ (Rom. 8:17). Quite appropriately, then, members addressed one another as "brother" and referred to themselves as "brethren."[2] Such love among themselves, a

---

1. The description of the church as the functioning "body" of Christ appears repeatedly in the New Testament. It is a figurative or metaphorical expression, and not to be interpreted literally as an extension of Christ's incarnation. An excellent discussion of the church in this image is by Stan Cole, *The Body of Christ* (London: Hodder & Stoughton, 1964). For a helpful treatment of other biblical figures used for the church, *see* Paul Minear, *Images of the Church in the New Testament* (Philadelphia: Westminster Press, 1970). More than eighty images are cited, though the focus is on the concepts of the body of Christ, people of God, the new Creation, and fellowship in faith. A more limited study, ably summarized, is by Robert L. Saucy, *The Church in God's Program* (Chicago: Moody Press, 1972), 19–56.

2. This term is used more than forty times in Acts alone. It describes persons who share a common heritage, like citizens of the same country, though it carries the additional force of brethren born of the same Spirit, when applied to Christians. *Note* 1:16; 6:3; 9:17; 10:23; 11:1, 12, 29; 12:17; 14:2; 15:1, 3, 23, 32, 33, 36, 40; 16:2, 40; 17:6,

quality derived from their Lord, became the seal of their witness to the world.[3] Christ had said: "By this shall all men know that ye are my disciples, if ye have love one to another" (John 13:35).

Unity in Diversity

Complimenting this love was a spirit of unity within the body (cf. John 17:21–23). The church in Jerusalem, numbering into the thousands, was "of one heart and soul" (4:32), a beautiful description of their solidarity. Again and again this community was said to be "with one accord" (2:46; 4:24; 5:12; 15:25). That they came to this oneness of mind in the meeting preceding Pentecost would indicate that unity provides a fertile soil for the Spirit of God to work (1:14; 2:1).

However, as the church expanded, their unity was threatened by internal division between the Hebrew Christians and new Gentile believers.[4] Some Judaizers

10, 14; 18:18, 27; 20:32; 21:7, 17, 20; 22:13; 28:14, 15, 17, 21, and others. The word also appears all through the letters of Paul and the General Epistles.

3. Gene A. Getz notes that this loving concern for one another is a concept that appears over fifty times in the Epistles alone, often in relation to church body life, e.g., Rom. 12:10, 16; 13:8; 14:10, 13; 15:5, 7, 14; 1 Cor. 12:25; Gal. 5:13; 6:2; Eph. 1:15; 4:1, 2, 32; 5:18–21; Col. 1:3, 4; 3:9, 12, 13, 16; 1 Thess. 3:12; 4:18; Heb. 3:13; 10:23–25; James 4:11; 5:9, 16; 1 Peter 1:22; 4:9; 5:5; 1 John 3:11, 23; 4:7, 11, 12; 2 John 5. *Sharpening the Focus of the Church* (Chicago: Moody Press, 1974), 115–116.

4. It is well to note that the church grew up in a Jewish system where already there was tension between contending factions, such as the Pharisees, Sadducees, Essenes, and Zealots. Each of these groups had its own distinctive cultural and theological emphases, though they shared a basic faith. So the rise of the Judiastic spirit in

insisted that all Gentile converts must adhere to their Jewish customs, particularly circumcision. It was not an easy problem to work through, even after God decisively intervened to get Peter and Cornelius together and confirmed their meeting by pouring out His Spirit upon them (10:1–48). The legalists still were dissatisfied, notwithstanding the evidence of God's direction (11:1–18). The issue came up again at the Jerusalem Council, where after rehearsing the previous events, all agreed that the church should not impose Jewish rites upon the Gentile Christians (15:1–29). Grace prevailed. Facing this question early in the life of the movement opened the way for the evangelization of the whole world. Had the narrow Judaizers won the day, Christianity would have become an ethnic rather than a universal faith.[5]

Not only was it recognized that God made "no distinction" between Jew and Gentile (15:9; cf. Eph. 2:14–18), but in the larger dimension of fellowship, every other artificial barrier to unity was broken down, whether of race, national origin, social and economic position, language, or sex. In the family of God, there was no Greek or barbarian, rich or poor, slave or free, male or female, but all were one in Christ (Col. 3:10, 11; Gal. 3:28).

---

the church was no reason to break fellowship with the Gentile Christians. Jews had already learned to live together amid diversity.

5. As a matter of historical interest, the Judaizers continued to maintain their position and create tension in the church. Paul's Letter to the Galatians, and to a lesser extent, his Letter to the Romans, speaks to the issues in this controversy. According to Eusebius, in A.D. 66 they left the Jerusalem church and went to Pella, where, removed from society, they followed their Jewish way of life. The community lost an evangelistic thrust and eventually faded away into oblivion. See Eusebius, The Ecclesiastical History, vol. 1 (Cambridge, Mass.: Harvard Univ. Press, 1926), 201.

Internal Tensions

This is not to imply that all was peaceful within the church. The Acts is careful to record continual problems coming up in the community. Early they had to deal with hypocritical members (5:1-11). As believers multiplied in Jerusalem, some Grecian Jews murmured because their widows were not receiving a fair distribution of provisions, a crisis that required swift administrative action (6:1-6). Then there were the tensions occasioned by lack of understanding and forgiveness, as seen in the hesitancy of the church to immediately accept Paul into the fellowship after his conversion (9:26). Though Barnabas resolved the problem (9:27), it did not prevent friction from developing later between Paul and John Mark (13:13); nor did it preclude contention even with Barnabas in the way Paul handled the situation (15:36-40).[6]

Paul's letters also mention internal strife in the churches, a situation the Corinthian congregation seemed most negligent about correcting. A member of that fellowship was living in open immorality. Some were taking each other to court over petty disputes. Disorders were occurring in the worship service. There were doctrinal differences and a tendency for people to take sides around strong, charismatic personalities. His letters reveal power struggles in other churches, including his own role of leadership. There are warnings against false teaching as well as synthesizing Christian and pagan customs. The General Epistles of James, Peter, and John indicate many

6. A good discussion of these internal problems in Acts may be found in C. E. Autrey, *Evangelism in Acts* (Grand Rapids, Mich.: Zondervan, 1964), 43-56.

of the same difficulties, as do the descriptions of the seven churches of Asia Minor, recorded in the Book of Revelation.

Clearly churches, even growing, vibrant congregations, have problems. If nothing else, just the sheer logistic pressure occasioned by a rapidly expanding fellowship precipitates tensions. When limited knowledge and spiritual immaturity—conditions always with us—are added to this, we can understand why problems constantly need resolution in the church. The issues need to be honestly faced and dealt with. To ignore them invites disaster. But to meet them in the sufficiency of God's grace makes the difficulties stepping-stones to progress. Essential to the reconciling process, however, is the mutual concern of the church, which allows problems to be addressed in the context of love.

Mutual Support

This willingness to bear one another's burdens is seen in their care of members with physical needs. It was like a family, where each person felt responsibility for the others. "And all that believed were together, and had all things common" (2:44). ". . . Not one of them said that aught of the things which he possessed was his own . . ." (4:32). To provide for those without the basic necessities of life, persons with means, like Barnabas, ". . . sold their possessions and goods, and parted them to all, according as any man had need" (2:45; cf. 4:34–37). The apostles distributed the provisions in an orderly manner, so that no one among them lacked (4:34; cf. 6:1).[7]

_____

7. The need for assistance was especially acute in this early period of the Jerusalem church, when Jewish believers were ostracized

This generous giving to brethren in need is noted again when the disciples at Antioch, "every man according to his ability," sent relief to the famine-stricken community in Judea (11:27–30). Paul, too, is a recipient of offerings from the churches concerned for his welfare (Phil. 4:15, 16). Mention also is made in his second letter to the Corinthians of the Macedonian churches being allowed to give money to the Jerusalem saints, even out of extreme poverty (2 Cor. 8:1–4).

Let it be stressed, however, that nothing in the common life of the church is compatible with the practice of materialistic socialism today. State communism is a legislated and forced sharing, imposed from the top down. By contrast, the apostolic church sees sharing as an individual choice, a consequence of love and self-denial, which comes from the bottom up. It is a spontaneous act of worship, giving as unto the Lord.

Corporate Meetings

The closeness of the church at Pentecost set the pattern. "They continued stedfastly in the apostles' teaching and fellowship, in the breaking of bread and the prayers" (2:42). Emphasis is upon a constancy of faith and devotion as they meet regularly for instruction, sharing of experiences and worship.[8]

---

from society, which deprived many of their economic support. The pressure was somewhat diminished as Christians moved out into the Gentile world.

8. The purpose of this study is not served by elaborating on the forms meetings took in the early church. Those who may be interested in pursuing this subject will find helpful the books by Oscar Cullman, *Early Christian Worship* (Naperville, Ill.: Allenson, 1953); Alexander R. Hay, *The New Testament Order for the Church and*

Specific information about the format of these meetings is not given, though it seems apparent that it was very simple. There was a time for reading the Scriptures (2:42; 15:21, 30, 31; Col. 4:16; 1 Thess. 5:27) and perhaps a sermon or exhortation, as was the custom in the synagogue (cf. 20:7, 17, 18). Of course, these meetings allowed for corporate prayer (1:14; 2:42; 4:24, 31; 12:5, 12; Rom. 12:10–13; 1 Thess. 5:14–18; James 5:13–16). From allusions to hymns and praise in the church, singing also seems to have been a part of the service (2:47; Eph. 5:19; Col. 3:16). In these spiritual songs the members edified one another, while expressing their love to God out of thankful hearts.

Normally, too, a fellowship meal, called the "agape" or "love feast" was observed, recalling the Last Supper of Christ with His disciples (2:42, 46; 20:7; 1 Cor. 10:16, 17). This practice led to abuses at Corinth, with some unworthy members using the meal for their own pleasure by overeating, an act Paul strongly reproved (1 Cor. 11:27–34). Properly observed, however, the sharing of their food and drink in remembrance of the Lord's passion was a beautiful experience of holy Communion.[9]

Mission (Audubon, Pa.: New Testament Missionary Union, 1947); Maurice Goguel, *The Primitive Church* (London: George Allen and Unwin, Ltd., 1963); and Ralph P. Martin, *Worship in the Early Church* (Westwood, N.J.: Fleming H. Revell, 1964). A shorter treatment is in Gary Inrig, *Life in His Body* (Wheaton, Ill.: Harold Shaw, 1975), esp. 66–100.

9. The common meal continued to be observed in the church for several centuries, though the practice gradually decayed, due largely to mixing the Christian purpose with worldly elements. It should be kept in mind, too, that while the table fellowship provided a relaxed setting for the Eucharist instituted by Christ, the meal was not a necessary part of the observance, which centered on the partaking of the

Throughout the meeting, ample opportunity seems to have been given for personal participation. Each believer was free to exercise his or her spiritual gift, ask questions, and share any concern, as the Spirit might lead. Officers in the local fellowship doubtless provided some direction to the service, but the worshipers were not dependent on them.

Worship patterns gradually became more formalized toward the close of the first century. The same trend was apparent in the development of catechisms and creeds, as well as the Communion meal, which took a more sacramental character. This is not to disparage formality or belittle the need for defining doctrine, for an increasingly complex body must have some stabilizing order. But in the formalizing process we must preserve the fellowship that gives heart to the structure.

Gathering Places

During this early period, the Christians did not have church buildings in which to meet. Those living in Jerusalem would gather in the temple area, especially at times of prayer (2:46; 3:1; 5:12, 21, 42), but this became difficult as Jewish opposition increased. The same pertained to the use of synagogues in other cities. Sometimes the Christians would assemble in the public halls that were available to them, as in "the upper chamber" at Troas (20:8), but

---

bread and the cup (1 Cor. 11:23–26). A good discussion of this whole practice is by J. F. Keating, *The Agape and the Eucharist in the Early Church* (New York: AMS Press, 1969). Also helpful is the succinct work of Dom Gregory Dix, *The Shape of the Liturgy* (London: Dacre Press, 1945), 48–102.

the use of such facilities does not appear to be a pattern.

Their normal place of meeting was in the home. The first gathering was in the upper chamber in the house of Mary, the mother of John Mark, which became a familiar prayer site for the brethren (1:13; 12:12). With the large increase in members, many houses in the city became meeting places for church groups (2:46). The home of Philip in Caesarea is mentioned as a rendezvous for the saints (21:8). A church met in the house of Philemon (Philem. 2). Jason's house in Thessalonica served the same purpose (17:5). At Corinth both the houses of Titus Justus and Stephanas were used as centers of fellowship (18:7; 1 Cor. 1:16). So also were the houses of Lydia, the jailer in Philippi (16:15, 32–34), and Nympha at Laodicea (Col. 4:15). Wherever Aquila and Priscilla move, it appears, too, that their house becomes a church site at Corinth, Ephesus, and Rome (18:26; 2 Tim. 4:19; 1 Cor. 16:19; Rom. 16:3, 5).

One has to ask, in all honesty, why did not the Christians erect special buildings for their corporate meetings, especially after leaving the synagogues? Not until near the end of the second century is there any record of a church edifice being constructed.[10] This stands in marked

---

10. To my knowledge, the earliest known church building was in Dura-Europos on the River Euphrates, where a house dating from A.D. 232 was adapted to make a larger assembly hall for worship. More recent discoveries have led some authorities to believe an earlier church edifice may have existed at Capernaum, perhaps in what was once the house of Peter. Interestingly, in both of these instances, the building seems to have been a renovated home. Colin J. Hemer, "Archaeological Light on Earliest Christianity," *The History of Christianity*, ed. Tim Dowley (Herts, England: Lion Publishing, 1977), 58; cf. Michael Green, *Evangelism in the Early Church* (Grand Rapids, Mich.: Wm. B. Eerdmans, 1970), 194.

contrast to the other religions of the time. Granted, permission to build may have been difficult to obtain in the hostile environment, though there were doubtless ways this problem could have been surmounted, at least, in friendly areas of the empire. Perhaps, too, costly building programs would have been hard to finance, with their limited resources. But it also seems probable that the Christians simply saw no compelling reason to erect buildings for worship. They were able to get along quite well without them.

Could there be a more natural setting for the meeting of Christian family? They gathered at home, where they lived their faith every day. In this relaxed atmosphere they learned together even as they shared one another's burdens. What better place could there be for the people of God to experience the closeness of their love?

Personal Relationships

The fellowship fostered in the church meetings was even more obvious in the daily relationships of Christians on the personal level. Reading the Acts, one gets the impression that the Christians just enjoyed doing things together. In these casual relationships, probably more than in their gathered meetings, they learned what it meant to follow Christ in the daily routine of life.

Much of this fellowship centered in home visitation (5:42). For example, attention is called to Peter's visit with Simon at Joppa, an occasion doubtless used to strengthen the tanner's faith (9:43; 10:6). The practice frequently comes out in Paul's ministry as he receives the hospitality of friends. In his case, not having a settled parsonage, it was a providential way for him to have his needs met, while also ministering to the needs of others.

His stay with Lydia and her family, after their conversion, is characteristic. Not only did Paul and Silas accept her invitation to abide in her house (16:15), but they returned later for a visit, following their release from prison (16:40). In the interval, after the conversion of the Philippian jailer, they stayed in his house, where the whole family came to Christ (16:34).

These visits with the brethren often were for extended periods. Sometimes they lasted for a few days (20:6, 7; 21:4, 7–10; 27:3; 28:7, 13, 14), at other times for many months. At Corinth he lived with Aquila and Priscilla for more than a year and a half (18:3, 11), establishing them in the faith, while also teaching the disciples meeting in Titus Justus's house (18:3, 7, 8, 11, 18, 19). Altogether Paul stayed with the Ephesian church three years (20:31) and nearly that long during his confinement in Rome, where Christians regularly came to visit him (28:30). The spiritual life of the Christian community clearly is interwoven with their continuous interpersonal association.

Traveling Together

Periods of travel were no interruption to fellowship. On his trip to Caesarea, we are told that Peter was accompanied by some of the Christians of Joppa, along with the three men who had come to seek him (10:7, 23, 45; 11:12). Likewise Paul, when persecution became intolerable in Damascus, was escorted by Barnabas to Jerusalem (9:27), then taken by the brethren to Caesarea (9:30). Later Barnabas brought him back to Antioch (11:26).

Moving about was a team exercise. As the narrative unfolds, the focus is upon the journeys of Paul and his

companions. But the principle of traveling together pertained to all the others, like Barnabas and Mark, Silas
and Timothy, and Timothy and Erastus. Frequently, too,
local brethren would join them (e.g. 21:15, 16). No less
than seven disciples were with Paul on his trip through
Macedonia, making it a mobile school (20:4).[11] Even
when Paul was a prisoner in transit to Rome, he was able
to have Aristarchus and Luke go with him (27:2–8; 28:1,
10–15). When finally they reached the city of Caesar,
brethren from the church came out to meet them, and
they walked into town together (28:15).

There was safety in numbers, of course. Marauding
robbers along the road made traveling in companies necessary for protection. But more important, it facilitated
fellowship in a natural setting. By teacher and pupil being
together, they were continually able to learn in the real
laboratory of the world. Whatever happened along the
way presented an occasion for teaching and reflection.
Though unassuming, it was a powerful experience of discipleship.

Follow-up of Believers

We can observe that all the way through there was a
special effort to bring new Christians, without delay, into
close relationships with other believers, both on the corporate and personal level. This way their growth was sus-

---

11. These men came from different areas of the world: Sopater
from Berea; Aristarchus and Secundus from Thessalonica; Gaius
and Timothy from Derbe; and Tychicus and Trophimus from Asia.
The special reference to their diverse homelands suggests that their
inclusion in the company had significance in the development of the
church. Probably they were training for leadership roles.

tained. The three thousand converts at Pentecost were immediately amalgamated into the church life, and this pattern continued daily with others as they were being saved (2:46, 47; 4:32). When the lame man is healed at the temple gate, Peter and John keep him with them as they continue their ministry (3:8; 4:14). With this same astuteness, the apostles in Jerusalem quickly dispatched Peter and John to the Samaritan believers when they heard that "Samaria had received the word of God" (8:14–25). Similar nurture was given by Peter to the household of Cornelius, following their reception of the Holy Spirit (10:48).

The emphasis given to Paul's follow-up after his conversion certainly underscores this need. Not only is he taken into a fellowship of disciples at Damascus, but he is joined by a man sent by God to give special instruction (9:8–19, 25). When taken later to Jerusalem, he remained with the apostles for a period of time, "going in and going out" among them (9:28). Doubtless Paul learned more during these days than the information he got from just knowing the leaders; he received an indispensable lesson in the care of new believers. For the rest of his life he made it a policy to stay with beginning disciples. He understood their need for personal follow-up, a desire that apparently they also felt, for believers sometimes "clave" to him (17:34), and "followed" him home, wanting to learn more of Christ (e.g. 13:43).

As they matured in the faith, he continued to relate to them as much as possible. Again and again he would go back to visit them, actually planning his missionary trips so that he could retrace much of the territory covered before. In these return calls he would meet with the church, "confirming the souls of the disciples, exhorting them to continue in the faith . . ." (14:21, 22). He was particularly anxious after each mission to spend time with the Christians at Antioch, where, having served on the church staff, he must have developed some deep roots, along with a sense of accountability (13:1-4; 14:27, 28; 15:30-35; 18:22).

When circumstances were such that he could not give the personal attention desired, he often arranged for others to take his place. Silas and Timothy, for example, were left behind at Berea when he had to leave (17:14); and Timothy and Erastus were sent into Macedonia in response to their urgent request, since he could not go himself (19:22). Such missions are alluded to repeatedly in his letters.

It is clear that in his deepening relationships Paul was conscious of a priority in spending time with persons training for leadership in the church. Hence much of his travels are in association with these maturing disciples. For example, Paul developed a close friendship with Priscilla and Aquila, with whom he stayed at Corinth (18:2, 3). There was a natural interest between them, in that they were fellow tentmakers. But more than that, they had a heart for God (Rom. 16:3). His hosts learned well, for when later Paul departed for Ephesus, taking this lovely couple with him, they did the same thing Paul had done with them—found a disciple, got with him, and patiently helped him know "the way of God more accurately" (18:19-26). It wasn't long before Apollos, in turn, went forth preaching Christ and helping others grow in grace (18:27, 28).

The letters of Paul reflect a personal concern for these growing leaders. Some sixty or more persons are mentioned by name in the Epistles. They are referred to as "friends," "partners," "fellow workers," "teammates," "faithful helpers," those who labored "side by side" with him. Obviously he had developed very close relationships with many of the brethren.

His farewell message to the elders of Ephesus, much like that of his follow-up letters, reflects this burden he carried for their development. Calling to mind how he was with them "all the time," he mentioned that he had faithfully taught them "publicly, and from house to house" everything that was profitable (20:18, 20). Nothing was withheld as he "ceased not to admonish" them "night and day with tears" (20:31). This is the concern of a loving father, zealous that his children in the faith attain to the full stature of Christ. The elders knew that his love for them was real, for when he had spoken, and prayed with them, "they all wept sore, and fell on Paul's neck and kissed him," knowing that they would see his face no more (20:36–38).

A Learning Fellowship

This relationship provided the environment for their training. The apostolic church did not erect colleges or theological seminaries, or even set up educational seminars. They had instruction in the tenets of the Christian faith and life, but not in formal classes or institutional programs. To mold the life of their members, they simply got learners and teachers together in natural settings, where they lived and worked every day.

Nothing was new in this approach. The church as the body of Christ was following the same approach to education as their Lord had used with His disciples. It is the principle of the family, by which most of our basic values are learned in this life. That is why all of us still reflect influences exerted upon us by our parents and other family members, especially in the formative years of early childhood.

Any effective method of education must incorporate this dynamic. It has been said that a college is a professor on one end of a log and a student on the other end. This may be an oversimplification, but we cannot miss the point. When all is said and done, our education will not be much better than our teachers, or the opportunity to learn much more than the way the teacher and student can be together.

This is what the apostolic church was doing in its development of disciples. In their community life, Christians developed an atmosphere conducive to growth. Questions could be asked and issues clarified without intimidation. Mutual trust existed. Whether in organized group meetings or informal friendly fellowship, the church translated theory into practice. To a remarkable degree, truth was demonstrated in real life. What they said and did was an object lesson in reality.

Nowhere was this more pronounced than in the beginning steps of persons just coming to Christ. These spiritual babes were immediately surrounded with love and made to feel a part of the family circle. No one could feel left out. Here was a community in which they all shared the bonds of an everlasting covenant.

Application Today

The implications of this upon the life of the church today dare not be missed. In our stress upon carefully ordered public services and organized campaigns, we may overlook the basic apostolic ingredient of fellowship.

Times have become more complex with the passing centuries, surely, but the principle of association never changes.

However structured, we must relate closely with one another. There are ways this can be encouraged in the regular worship services, even in formal, sacramental settings. Auxiliary meetings offer other opportunities for fellowship, especially in small-group gatherings. In this connection, the Sunday school provides many options. Emphasis must be given to the home and family in the program. Through it all, personal relationships need continual cultivation in the ongoing discipling process.

This is crucial in helping new believers get established. In their first steps of faith, they are particularly vulnerable to doubts and temptations and need someone with them to give counsel. How fortunate when this person can be a more mature Christian with whom they already have some identity. That the church has often neglected such guardian care explains why so many converts fall away or at least never seem to grow in the likeness of their Lord.

Maturing in Christ takes time. There is no way that children can be raised in a hurry. To try to get it over quickly can only lead to frustration. The hectic way that churches have tried to force this into a few weeks of confirmation classes, if they have done it at all, is entirely inadequate. Disciples must have devoted Christian friends to follow, and this can only be facilitated by being together over a period of time.

This establishes the foundation for dynamic learning. But it must not be isolated from a caring ministry to the world. To bring this aspect of the Great Commission into focus, we must study another principle of discipleship.

4

The Ministry to Give

A Ministering Community

The first-century church body existed for ministry. Every member of the community shared the servant role of their Lord and, in the way He appointed, continued His mission on earth. As Paul expressed it, they were ambassadors of Christ, ministering in His stead (2 Cor. 5:20).

In the sense of being sent into the world on a mission, all believers became successors to the apostles or "sent ones."[1] This does not depreciate the special apostolic gift;

---

1. The word *apostle* denotes one sent, as on an official mission, and in this general sense, refers to any follower of Christ (e.g. John 17:18; 20:21). Used in the sense of divine appointment, the term

it merely underscores a basic Christian obligation to per-
petuate the apostolic witness (2:42). The early church recognized their inherent responsibility and accepted it with
gladness. That some in the fellowship might be excused
from service does not even occur as an option. All saw
themselves as workers together with Christ in reconciling
the world to God.[2] It was the mobilization of this growing
force of laborers that made the apostolic community so
mighty in outreach.

Differing Gifts

Not all served in the same way, of course. There were
many different forms of ministry, depending upon the

---

might be translated "missionary." From this perspective, it can be
said that all believers participate in the apostolic succession and are
sent forth by Christ as missionaries. However, in the more restricted
sense, apostles were those persons specially commissioned to plant
churches through the preaching of the Gospel and to build up congregations in matters of doctrine and government. The office was
held with great importance, and it is mentioned first in connection
with God's gifts to the church (Eph. 4:11; 1 Cor. 12:28). The term
may denote the twelve (e.g. 1:15–26; 2:37, 43; 4:33; Luke 22:30; Heb.
3:1; Rev. 21:14), Paul (1 Cor. 9:1, 2; 15:5–9; 2 Cor. 12:11, 12), Barnabas (14:4), Apollos or Sothenes (1 Cor. 4:9), Andronicus and Junia
(Rom. 16:7), Silvanus and Timothy (1 Thess. 2:6; cf. 1:1), and others
(1 Cor. 15:5–7). What has come to be known as "apostolic succession" was a theory that did not originate until late in the second
century. At that point it was a useful means by which the church
sought to combat heresy by making bishops custodians of the apostolic teaching. *See* Everett F. Harrison, *The Apostolic Church* (Grand
Rapids, Mich.: Wm. B. Eerdmans, 1985), 151–154.

2. This might explain why the church did not choose successors to
the twelve after Pentecost. At least there is no mention of someone
being selected to replace James after his martyrdom (12:2). Did the
church now see that the apostolic mission, distinguished from the
gift of apostle, belonged to them all, so there was no need to keep the
place of the twelve intact?

abilities and qualifications given by God (Rom. 12:6-8; 1
Cor. 12:4-11, 28-30; Eph. 4:7-12; 1 Pet. 4:10). Whether
these traits were natural talents brought under divine
control or special endowments resulting from the operation of the Spirit within the believer's life, they evidenced
a sovereign grace.

Some of these gifts prepared Christians with basic
inner motivations for declaring God's truth, serving practical needs, teaching and clarifying facts, exhorting believers concerning the application of truth, entrusting
money and possessions to others, administering activities,
and empathizing with the distress of people. Some gifts
related to a special ministry needed in the church, which
might be that of missionary, preacher, explainer of the
Scriptures, worker of miracles, healer, helper, adminis-
trator, speaker in various kinds of tongues, evangelist, or
pastor. Still other gifts enabled one to restore hope by receiving a word of wisdom, distinguishing between spirits,
interpreting tongues, or something else necessary to redeem a life situation. The listings of Paul were probably
not intended to be exhaustive, but only suggestive of the
various ways that God enables the church to fulfill His
calling.[3]

---

3. Much has been said about spiritual gifts in recent years, not
without controversy. Nevertheless, it is a matter that cannot be ignored in considering the ministry of the church. Some are of the
opinion that the gifts, or at least some of them, passed away with the
apostolic age. Scriptural support for this position, at best, is very
tentative. To contend that these endowments of grace would cease
with the death of the original apostles or even after the first few centuries seems arbitrary to me and, I think, lacks objective support.
Not only did gifts continue to be manifest through the history of the
church, especially in times of spiritual awakening, but they are in
evidence today. That there have been misrepresentations of the
teaching should not distract us from seeking the truth.

Obviously some Christians, like Paul, were more gifted than others. The number and strength of gifts, however, establishes no merit or superiority. It would seem that disciples were not responsible for the possession of gifts, but for their use. For example, wrongly related, spiritual knowledge may puff up (1 Cor. 8:1), just as the gift of tongues may lead to self-glory (1 Cor. 14:2). Like any true blessing, the gifts can be misused and falsified. Such abuse met with strong reproof by the church (e.g. 8:18–24; 19:13–16).

The purpose of God's gifts must always be kept in view. They are given, not to foster pride in recipients but to perfect the body of Christ and thereby bring glory to God. When exercised within this intention, there is personal fulfillment, and the whole body benefits. Love is the supreme fruit. It shines through the harmonious operation of the gifts as well as the result of their effective function (1 Cor. 13:1–13; Eph. 4:16).

Equipping the Saints

In the economy of God's design, some of these gifted persons are prepared for particular roles of leadership in the church. Apostles served as foundation builders, sent in a missionary capacity (e.g. 15:6). Prophets proclaim the message of God, an office almost comparable to preaching (e.g. 15:32; 21:8, 9). Evangelists were particularly gifted in speaking to the lost (8:5–8; 21:8; 2 Tim. 4:5). Pastors were overseers and shepherds of the flock (e.g. 20:28), an office closely associated, if not identical to, that of teacher (e.g. 11:26; 13:1).

These persons were in a unique position to equip the

church for the work of ministry that they shared together (Eph. 4:11, 12).[4] It was not their place to do all the labor themselves, but rather to train the people for the task committed by Christ to His whole body. By so doing, the members of the church are built up to a place of strength and maturity, until all become full-grown in the Lord (Eph. 4:13).

What a contrast this is to the idea prevalent today that the pastor and the church staff are employed by a congregation to take care of ministry needs. That may well be what the people think they are paying the professional workers for, but it surely betrays a tragic misunderstanding of the believer's role of service. Where this perverted notion exists, those who are in a privileged teaching position must take initiative in correcting the situation. The place to begin is with the officers of the assembly.

Leadership Offices

The church of Acts sets us a good example in leadership administration. At first the twelve apostles managed things in Jerusalem by assuming general oversight of the brethren (4:37; 5:12, 42). But when the size of the congregation increased to such proportions that the daily administration of physical details became overwhelming, they realized that the leadership base had to be increased. So calling the people together, the twelve asked the congregation to select "seven men of good report, full of the Spirit and of wisdom" to whom they could delegate some of their work load. With the growing demands of the

---

4. See my note on this passage in *The Master Plan of Evangelism* (Old Tappan, N.J.: Fleming H. Revell, 1964), 34.

church, their time for prayer and the ministry of the Word, a priority they dared not compromise, was being squeezed. The apostles' proposal met with favor. Seven men were chosen by the people, then officially inducted into the office by the apostles' laying on of hands (6:1–6).[5]

This marks the beginning of what came to be called the diaconate (Phil. 1:1; 1 Tim. 3:8). Generally designating servants of God (e.g. John 12:26; Luke 8:2, 3), the term developed a more specialized reference to persons engaged in oversight of temporal matters in the church. Precedent for the office had already been established with the synagogue workers who collected and distributed alms. Deacons did more than distribute food, though to relieve the apostles of this task, their responsibility started with this ministry. In time deacons served a wide range of needs, like caring for the poor and infirm, providing instruction, as well as management of church business affairs. Before being ordained to this work, they were to be "proved," suggesting that their conduct had to demonstrate exemplary character (1 Tim. 3:8–13). Timothy and Phoebe are mentioned as persons in this position (1 Tim. 4:6; Rom. 16:1).

As the church expanded and the apostles started to

---

5. Here is a beautiful example of conflict management. Note how the leaders were honest with the people, not only in expressing their own frustrations, but also in sharing their perception of the people's complaint. By recognizing the situation at this early stage, too, they were able to deal with the problem before it became a calamity. They did not attempt to do it alone, but rather called the congregation together, focused the issue, offered some counsel, then let the people decide what course to take. Though the idea for the solution came from the apostles, they wisely let the congregation own it, after which they put their seal of approval upon the people's choice. In so doing they maintained control of the situation without dictating policy, gaining support of the people for their leadership, while also maintaining their own personal spiritual priorities.

move out of Jerusalem, elders appeared in the leadership of the home congregation (11:30; cf. 15:2, 4, 6, 22, 23; 16:4; 21:18). How this position was inaugurated is not explained, but it had antecedents in Israel, where elders constituted the governing council of the Jews (e.g. 4:5, 8, 23; 6:12). Following this tradition, elders in the church were "overseers" or "bishops" of the believers in their locality. They had a special teaching responsibility "to feed the church" (20:28; Titus 1:5–8) and to exercise pastoral oversight of "the flock" among them (1 Pet. 5:2).[6] It was not their duty to minister on behalf of the members, but to supervise and encourage the work belonging to them all. Those who ruled well and labored faithfully in the work and doctrine were worthy of honor (1 Tim. 5:17). Though their leadership did not engender dependence, it did invoke respect.

Elders were appointed in each congregation as churches were established (14:23; 20:17; Titus 1:5; James 5:14; 1 Pet. 5:1). The selection was based on the church's perception of their spiritual maturity and competence as well as the sense of God's special calling.[7] Unless they happened to have another office, like that of an apostle, they did not travel from church to church, but remained

6. The words for *elder*, or *bishop*, and *overseer* or *presbyter* are synonyms and can be used interchangeably in the New Testament. By the end of the first century the title *bishop* began to be applied to a single leader of the church, but this distinction arises entirely out of tradition, not the Scriptures. An excellent treatment of this term will be found in Bishop Lightfoot's commentary, *Saint Paul's Epistle to the Philippians* (Grand Rapids, Mich.: Zondervan, 1953), 95–99.

7. In a general way, those who respond to the Gospel invitation are the called (e.g. Rom. 1:16). But in the more specialized sense, the call of God may relate to the vocation of a person, such as a missionary, or an office like that of elder. The perception of a call involves sensitivity to the leading of the Spirit, both on the part of the individual and the church (e.g. 13:1–4).

in the church out of which they came. Significantly, too, the word normally appears in the plural, indicating that there were multiple elders in a church. This prevented congregations from coming under the control of a single personality and accented the body principle of a shared ministry even in leadership. What has already been observed in the team travels of the missionaries found its counterpart in the churches they established.

The Servant Example

But how could this arrangement survive the diverse makeup of personalities, with all the variations of interest? The answer lies not in ignoring the ever-present possibility of conflict, but in recognizing the authority of Christ, who was the Head of the church. Whatever differences there were between persons—differences that often caused tension—there was the overriding consciousness that all were responsible to a greater authority.

With Jesus as the supreme example to follow, servanthood became the rule of His body. There was no place for an authoritarian stance among the leaders, for all were under the Lordship of Christ. No one could dictate the behavior of others. Differences in gifts and styles were complementary, not competitive. What made it possible was brotherly love, "in honor preferring one another" (Rom. 12:10). Those who led were first of all servants, a quality nowhere more essential than in relationships with fellow leaders.

Persons in official positions were expected to be "ensamples to the flock" (1 Pet. 5:3). Speaking of the elders and deacons, Paul said they were to be blameless in character, gentle, upright, not quarrelsome or arrogant or

lovers of money, hospitable, vigilant, not given to strong
drink. Particularly important was the inviolate relationships of husband and wife, as well as the way their children were submissive and respectful, for if leaders cannot
manage their own house, how can they rule the church?
As to doctrine, they were to be ready to teach, "holding
the mystery of the faith in a pure conscience." Even those
outside the fellowship should speak well of them (1 Tim.
3:1–13).

Example gives credibility to leadership. People are far
more impressed by what they see than what they hear.
Paul reminded the elders of Ephesus how he had kept
back nothing that was for their good and had "showed"
them all things (20:20, 35). Writing to the church at Philippi, he said: "The things which ye both learned and received and heard and saw in me, these things do ..."
(Phil. 4:9). He did not invite disciples to follow a theory,
but a person. That person was Jesus Christ, the only Lord
and Savior. But they were to follow Christ as Paul followed Him (1 Cor. 11:1). The apostle's life was not the
end of their quest, but it was an example of one seeking
with all his heart and soul to be a disciple of Christ (Phil.
3:17; 1 Thess. 2:8; 2 Tim. 1:13; cf. John 13:15).

Flexible Church Structure

As ministering groups of believers multiplied, their
common faith and practice were encouraged through the
visitations and writings of the apostles. The increasing diversity of peoples within the church, with the attendant
tensions, precipitated the need for leaders across the

church to work through the difficulties, as they did at the Jerusalem Council. Local congregations recognized the decisions of this body—agreements that were recorded and circulated throughout the churches (15:22–29). However, apart from the Scriptures, there was no binding ecumenical voice. Authority in world relations was spiritual, not official.

Church government in the New Testament centers in the local body of believers. Organization was simple, largely evolving around the leadership of elders and deacons and the exercise of equipping gifts. Generally polity developed a congregational form, patterned after the Jewish synagogue. These communities of disciples were fraternally related to other congregations, but internally managed their own affairs. Gradually, the church assimilated norms of the Roman world, organizing congregations into dioceses, with oversight of bishops. The basic ingredient of parish ministry was unchanged, though it had absorbed the structure of its culture, a practice quite compatible with the church philosophy of ministry.

Very early another structure conditioned by its environment grew up; Ralph Winter calls it "the apostolic bands."[8] Self-supporting and largely independent operations, these select missionary teams had their roots in the practices of Jewish proselytizers. From this "order" evolved many of the later renewal movements and "parachurch" organizations.

---

8. This concept is discussed by Ralph Winter in "The Anatomy of the Christian Mission," *Evangelical Mission Quarterly*, vol. 2 (Winter, 1969): 74–89. *Also see* his "The Two Structures of God's Redemptive Mission," *Crucial Dimensions of World Evangelization* (Pasadena, Calif.: Wm. Carey Lib., 1976).

The church's policy of pragmatism encouraged creativity. The rule seemed to be: Within the guidelines of the apostles' teaching, whatever facilitates the ministry, do it. This gave them freedom to experiment with new ventures and to utilize the patterns of their society when they could be effectively incorporated into the life of the church. At the same time, no particular form was canonized. What is important is that the most helpful means be found in every setting to accomplish the task at hand.

Variable Methods of Witnessing

Following this philosophy, members of the apostolic church employed many different methods in seeking to reach their contemporaries with the Gospel. Preaching was certainly one of the more prominent modes of evangelism.[9] Seemingly, wherever a crowd could be gathered, the opportunity was seized to proclaim the Word of God. Having no church buildings of their own, they used other facilities, like assembly areas of the temple and the synagogues. However, more sermons are recorded in nonreligious settings, as in the open air on street corners or Mars Hill, family dwellings, judgment halls, and a prison in Rome.

The preaching usually developed out of a preceding event, becoming an explanation of the occurrence, like interpreting the phenomena of Pentecost or responding to a mob awed by the miracle at Lystra. The composition of

---

9. A good discussion of the public forms of evangelical preaching may be found in Michael Green, *Evangelism in the Early Church* (Grand Rapids, Mich.: Wm. B. Eerdmans, 1970), 194–207.

the audience, it would seem, largely determines how sermonic proof material is utilized. To Jews, for example,
strong use is made of scriptural authority. To pagans, natural revelation is used more freely. One cannot help but
be impressed with the relevance of the messages to the
immediate situation.

In the larger context of Christian communication, the
manner of speaking varies considerably, with delivery
moving from bold proclamation to casual conversation.
Preaching and personal witnessing are so related that, in
many instances, a distinction between the two cannot be
made. The same could be said of teaching.[10] Actually, of
the various terms used for some form of speech in Acts,
few convey a sermonic image[11] Those occurring most

---

10. A careful treatment of this blending in early Christianity is by
R. C. Worley in his *Preaching and Teaching in the Early Church*
(Philadelphia: Westminster Press, 1967). Dr. Worley takes exception
to C. H. Dodd's book, *The Apostolic Preaching and Its Developments*
(London: Hodder & Stoughton, 1936), which makes an arbitrary sep-
aration between the *kerygma* (preaching) and the *didache* (teaching).

11. Thirty-one terms in the Greek are found in Acts for Christian
verbal communication, and altogether they are used about 160 times.
Of these, the words *evangelize* or *preach* the Gospel (ἐναγγελίζω),
proclaim (κηρύσσω), *announce*, (καταγγέλλεω), *testify* (μαρτυρέω),
speak boldly (παρῥηψίς), *speak freely* (παρρησιάζομαι), and *prophesy*
(προφητέω) suggest what might be thought of as formal delivery. Yet
they represent less than a third of all the usages of speaking words.
The other terms are *teach* (διδάσκω), *reason* (διαλέγομαι), *exhort*
(παρακαλέω), *answer* (ἀπεκρινάτο), *speak* (φθέγγομαι), *charge*
(παραγγέλλω), *ministrate* (διακόνω), *prove* (συμβιβάζω), *confound*
(συγχέω), *relate* (διάγω), *expound* (ἐξετίθιτα), *confirm* (στηρίζω), *explain* (διανοίγω), *persuade* (πείθω), *confute utterly* (δακατελέγχω),
greet (ἀσπάζομαι), *address* (προσφωνέω), *speak in defense* (ἀπο-
λογέομαι), *admonish* (παραινέω), *draw out* (συνεξερύω), *set forth*
(παρατίθεμουσ), *cry out* (ἐκράξεν), *talk* (λαλέω) and *say* (λέγω). Many

commonly are simply the words *talk* and *say*. This accents again the ordinary communication of the believers, most of whom do not feel competent or gifted in the area of public speaking. But anyone redeemed by grace can say a good word for Jesus, whenever the occasion seems appropriate.

Personal Evangelism

In this area of personally sharing their faith, leaders of the church set a good example. Peter and John were quick to make the physical need of a handicapped man an occasion to speak of Jesus (3:1–16). Later they are seen dealing forthrightly with Simon of Samaria (8:9–24). Philip is depicted not only as a preacher of Christ to the people (8:5), but also a personal witness to the Ethiopian eunuch on the road to Gaza (8:26–40). Paul confronts Elymas, and though the sorcerer remains hostile, the missionary's bold manner leads Sergius, the chief deputy of Cyprus, to believe (13:6–12). By the riverbank at Philippi, Paul wins Lydia to the Savior and in turn reaches her household (16:13–15). The Name of Christ is invoked over a demon-possessed girl in the same city (16:16–18). When Paul and Silas are thrown into jail for their upsetting ministry, the jailer and his family are converted through direct testimony (16:19–40). It appears that Cris-

---

words are used in references to both ordained church spokesmen and unordained believers. This raises an interesting question in regard to what usage pertains to a call to preach. Since there are thirty-one words in Acts that indicate speaking, one has to ask which word for speaking is meant. What would distinguish that form of preaching from the speech of any other member of the church?

pus, the chief ruler of the Jews in Corinth, along with others, is led to Christ in his house, after leaving the synagogue (18:7, 8). Aquila and Priscilla are influenced by the personal work of Paul (18:1-4), and they in turn instruct Apollos in the way of the Lord (18:24-28). Paul deals personally with the disciples of John at Ephesus (19:1-7), and he is seen sharing his testimony with the sailors on his voyage to Rome (27:9-44). Clearly the Book of Acts wants us to realize that these early leaders were no less astute in personal evangelism than they were in formal preaching, an example that should not go unnoticed by pulpiteers today.

But the ministry of the leaders, while the focus of Acts, was only exemplary of a general apostolic responsibility. The pattern emerges at Pentecost, when the Spirit-filled members go to the streets and declare "the mighty works of God" (2:1-11). Peter later preached and gathered the three thousand converts, but all the hundred and twenty had been out witnessing to the people. I suspect that if our congregations now were as zealous in telling the Gospel as those first disciples, then we, too, would see amazing response when an invitation is given by the preacher.

The same compulsion to speak the Word of God with boldness follows the outpouring of the Spirit upon the church prayer meeting in Jerusalem (4:31). Here we are specifically told that a "multitude" was involved (4:32). When persecution came during the tribulation that arose around Stephen, many of the Christians left Jerusalem and "scattered" throughout the regions of Judea and Samaria, "except the apostles" (8:1).[12] It was the parishioners, not the select apostles, who initially went forth as

---

12. Why the apostles remained in Jerusalem at this time is not explained. Some have conjectured that they were needed to assist in

evangelizers of the world. Everywhere they "were scattered abroad," they "went about preaching the word" (8:4). The term used here, literally meaning "evangelizing" or "bringing the good tidings," is the same word used of the apostles elsewhere. The whole church was preaching the Gospel. Some of them traveled as far as Phoenicia, Cyprus, and Antioch, "speaking the word" only to the Jews (11:19), while others, men from Cyprus and Cyrene, "spake unto the Greeks also, preaching the Lord Jesus" (11:20).

Out of the church that they established at Antioch came the missionary travels of Paul and others. With the planting of new congregations in metropolitan centers and the ordination of their leaders, believers who were being trained in the faith began to evangelize the area about them. Thus Paul could write to the church of the Thessalonians: "From you hath sounded forth the word of the Lord, not only in Macedonia and Achaia, but in every place your faith to God-ward is gone forth . . ." (1 Thess. 1:8). That is why, after many believed the preaching of Paul at Antioch of Pisidia, "the word of the Lord was spread abroad throughout all the region" (13:49). In the same way, after two years of Paul's reasoning among the

---

writing the Gospels. Others surmise that perhaps they took wives (1 Cor. 9:5) and therefore were limited in travel. More probable is that they stayed to give direction to the growing church, even in the face of persecution, until leadership could be raised up to take their place. Gradually the twelve move out of the city, where we might assume that they established churches. The last mention of the twelve in Jerusalem is at the council (15:1–29), but by this time, James the brother of Jesus has become the dominant leader of the home church (12:17; Gal. 1:19). An interesting treatment of the apostles' reluctance to leave Jerusalem is by Don Richardson, "The Hidden Message of Acts," in *Perspectives on the World Christian Movement,* ed. Ralph D. Winter and Steven C. Hawthorne (Pasadena, Calif.: Wm. Carey Lib., 1981), 89–99.

disciples at Ephesus, ". . . all they that dwelt in Asia heard the word of the Lord, both Jews and Greeks." (19:10). The apostle was in the city teaching and setting an example of witnessing before the church, but the real evangelizing of the area came through those persons Paul was discipling, who in turn were reaching others.

Reproduction through discipling is the pattern of the evangelistic explosion all through the Acts. Though attention centers upon a few leading spirits who are setting the pace, the real work of multiplication comes through the steady, unpretentious, faithful witness of the brethren. Meetings for fellowship, worship, and studying were just the catalyst for church outreach. It was in the marketplaces, the shops, along the streets and alleyways, where the people lived and worked every day, that the world was being turned upside down.

Centrality of the Home

Nowhere was this more evident than in Christians' homes. Here, where friendships are most natural and genuine, evangelism centered. Going from "house to house" seemed to be a pattern of church visitation (5:42; 20:20). Special attention is given to reaching the head of a house, who, when convinced of the claims of Christ, becomes the means of winning the family, as with the Philippian jailer (16:25–34). In the case of Cornelius, his household included not only relatives, but friends and servants (10:7, 22–48). With Lydia, probably an unmarried woman supporting a household, the slaves or freedmen in the house followed her example in the faith (16:14, 15). One can imagine, too, the influence of godly parents upon their children in the home, bringing them at an early age to embrace the Savior (e.g. 2 Tim. 1:5).

Strangers who came into their houses, also, could not escape the witness, as with Apollos, when he stayed with Aquila and Priscilla (18:24–26). Even in pagan homes there were opportunities for witness among Christian servants and guards, as in "Caesar's household" (Phil. 4:22; cf. 1:13).

The emphasis on evangelism invariably comes back to the church people, young and old, together and individually, living out their faith where they are and making disciples in the most natural way according to their gifts. It was the privilege of the whole body, and it could be done all the time. Witnessing was not a technique or a program, but a life-style.[13]

Signs and Wonders

Reinforcing the spoken word and contributing to its impact was a compassionate ministry to people's bodily suffering, a concern often attended with miraculous acts of healing. The lame man at the gate called Beautiful is an example (3:1–10). What happened with this beggar was not an isolated incident, for we are told many other "wonders and signs were done through the apostles" (2:43; 5:12), and many were added to the church (5:14). So great was the fame of Peter in this ministry that people brought their sick to the streets and laid them on couches, hoping that at least the shadow of the apostle might fall upon them, with the result that "they were healed every

13. The limits of this study prevent going into the details of personal witnessing in the New Testament, but it is a subject that has been developed in a limited way by other authors. *See* G. Campbell Morgan, *The Great Physician* (Old Tappan, N.J.: Fleming H. Revell, 1937), 329–400; and Faris D. Whitesell, *Basic New Testament Evangelism* (Grand Rapids, Mich.: Zondervan, 1949), 111–124.

one" (5:15, 16). Aeneas, a man sick of palsy, was healed at Lydda, and all that saw him "turned to the Lord" (9:35). At Joppa, Dorcas was resurrected from the dead after she had already been prepared for burial, resulting in many conversions (9:36–42). Similar works were seen in the ministry of Stephen (5:8) and Philip (8:6, 7, 13), with the same response by the onlookers. Likewise, healings are mentioned frequently during the ministry of Paul (14:3, 10–12; 15:12; 16:16–18; 19:11, 12; 20:7–12; 28:8, 9). Diseased bodies were made whole; unclean spirits were cast out of the possessed; the dead were raised.

A supernatural atmosphere pervaded the Christian witness. It was manifest in the phenomena attending Pentecost (2:1–4), in the earthquake while the church prayed (4:31), in deliverances from prison by angels (5:19; 12:10), in special revelations from heaven (10:3, 9–22, 46; 11:15, 18), in protection from the deadly sting of serpents (28:3–6), in judgment upon antagonists (12:23; 13:11, 12), and in the startling phenomena attending the conversion of their chief persecutor (9:3–9, 17, 18). Clearly there was a miraculous character about the apostolic community, preeminently evidenced in the changed lives of redeemed sinners. In basic nature, every true Christian is a continuous walking miracle.

One must always keep this inner dimension of personal transformation in view when considering the effect of miracles, especially physical healings. The more visible manifestations served to confirm the spoken word and to announce that the Messianic age had come,[14] but they

---

14. From of old it was expected that healings would accompany the joyful flourishing of Christ's kingdom. As Isaiah said: "Then the eyes of the blind shall be opened, and the ears of the deaf shall be unstopped. Then shall the lame man leap as a hart, and the tongue of

were never intended to supersede the primary spiritual ministry of the church. What God does in contravening His natural laws is not intended to exalt the flesh, but to show His own glory, finally revealed in the Son, which by His grace is displayed in the character of His saints. When this purpose is clear, ministry to the body certainly complements care for the soul. That is why healing and evangelism flow together beautifully in the apostolic church.

Physical distress cannot be ignored when seeking to meet the spiritual needs of mankind. Body and spirit are so entwined that they cannot be easily separated. Jesus recognized this wholeness of need as He ministered to the total human being. The charge given His disciples to preach the Gospel also included authority to heal the sick and cast out demons (Mark 3:14, 15; 6:7; 16:15–18; Matt. 10:1; Luke 9:1). It makes sense to believe that if God can redeem persons from iniquity, He can take care of physical afflictions as well. Indeed, within the church, praying for the sick among the early Christians was seen as much their privilege as asking for forgiveness of sins (James 5:14, 15).[15] A ministry that lacks this concern may seem distant, if not irrelevant, to suffering persons.

Meeting the Needs of Society

The early church could not ignore the needs of the poor, the sick, the blind, widows, and orphans, espe-

---

the dumb shall sing. . . . And a highway shall be there, and a way, and it shall be called The way of holiness'' (Isaiah 35:5, 6, 8).

15. I am not implying that the Lord will always heal as requested, for He may have other ends in view, knowing what is best for His people. But every believer has the right to appeal for healing according to the will of God.

cially those of their own body. But these people were
ministered to personally. One might wonder why more attention was not given to crusading against the massive oppression of their society. What about the entrenched evils
of the social and political system in which they lived—
slavery, degradation of women, child marriage, exploita-
tion of cheap labor, corruption in government, and
countless other injustices of their day? Surely the Christians were aware of these affronts to human dignity, for
they were themselves among the most victimized by the
structures.

Yet the institutional depravity about them does not
seem of primary concern. Just as their Lord, they are occupied with a greater vision. The coming of the Kingdom
through the transforming power of the Gospel is the burden of their witness, quite in contrast to the pronouncements of some church councils today. The Acts gives us
a lesson in realism, showing how to effect genuine and
lasting social change by dealing with the root cause of sin,
not mere symptoms of the problem.

Let no one imagine, however, that this focus minimizes
social responsibility. Persons with a Gospel priority cannot be indifferent to the cry for justice across the world,
and many, by virtue of their calling, will take leading
roles in shaping public policy. Whether one serves as a
politician or itinerant evangelist makes no difference, for
in any honorable vocation and through whatever gift one
may have, there will be opportunity to minister for Christ.

Application Today

A church that brings this sense of mission into the ev-
eryday life of her people will change the world for

good, for more and more redeemed sinners will live by the values of the world to come. Merely restructuring social programs without changing the perverted life-style of persons who participate in them does not produce righteousness or give people real peace and joy. The ultimate need of a lost society cannot be met apart from supernatural grace and the discipling of men and women in the narrow way of Christ.

At this most basic level of human need the fellowship of believers share a common ministry. Everyone according to his or her gifts has a part in changing the course of history. Those in institutional leadership positions may have more influence in setting policy, but no more authority in making disciples. The Great Commission is a personal matter. How the programs of the church prepare members for this servanthood is the measure of their relevance—meetings, committees, crusades, retreats, training sessions, parties, schools, service projects—everything must contribute to the mission for which we are sent into the world.

If this criterion were applied to our present religious activity, I wonder how much of it would be worth the effort. Somewhere in our rush of services, I am afraid that we have substituted institutional programs for our own priesthood. Pomp and ceremony all too often have stifled creativity and individual expression. Tradition has taken precedence over the guidelines of Scripture. We must get back to the apostolic norm of ministry and mobilize the whole body of Christ for action.

This is how the Gospel of the Kingdom will reach the ends of the earth. But the work will not be completed without personal sacrifices. To appreciate what this means, it is necessary to understand another vital principle in the life of the victorious church.

5

The Discipline to Keep

Living Faith

Pagan religions of the ancient world usually separated belief and conduct in a fashion unknown to first-century Christianity. The priests and priestesses of the ancient idols did not insist on a change of behavior; rather devotees of the pagan religions could live much as they pleased.[1]

---

1. The cultish religions of the ancient world imposed pompous acts of obeisance upon their adherents, like initiation rituals of abstinence and offering oblations to the gods, but there was no insistence upon a complete change of behavior. Many people, in fact, did not

In contrast, coming to Christ in the early church constituted an engagement of one's total personality and lifestyle. Those who believed were persons "obedient to the faith" (6:7).[2] God gave His spiritual powers "to them that obey him" (5:32; cf. 5:36, 37). Clearly faith involved far more than an intellectual assent to the historical validity of Christ's work; as Jesus had said, it was a commitment to follow Him—to walk in His steps (10:43; 13:12, 39, 48; 15:11; 17:12; 28:24). Appropriately, then, Christianity came to be described as "the Way" (9:2; 19:9, 23; 22:4; 24:14, 22; cf. 16:17; 18:25).

Followers of this Way were called disciples. They were recognized by their devotion to the Master, evidenced by obedience to His precept and example. That is why they were ever growing in grace and knowledge. Disciples are teachable because they want to learn. It is no accident that believers in the Book of Acts, as well as the Gospels, are often identified by this term.[3] Of course, they also

---

even believe on the contrived deities, though in deference to public expectations, they went through the accepted forms of worship. *See* Michael Green, *Evangelism in the Early Church* (Grand Rapids, Mich.: Wm. B. Eerdmans, 1970), 144–148, 315.

2. Faith and obedience were also joined in true Judaism. It was the unlawful division between them that led to Israel's degeneration. Had the fathers truly obeyed the Spirit, they would not have rejected the prophets or the promised Savior of whom they spoke (7:39, 51–53).

3. Believers are described as *disciples* 32 times in the Acts, while the term is applied to them more than 200 times in the Gospels. Interestingly, however, it is not used in the Epistles. Perhaps this could be due to the different focus of the books. In the essentially historical narratives. where action is so prominent, the designation of *disciple* seems more appropriate; while in the Letters, where doctrinal interpretation takes precedent, words like *saint* and *elect* (which have more theological overtones) come to mind.

came to be called Christians (11:26), which was not strange, since persons inevitably take on the character of the One they follow.

Facilitating the learning process was discipline, a quality inherent in discipleship. In fact, both words are derived from the same root. Sincere disciples of Christ accept His rules of conduct, as in a school, bringing every thought into obedience to their Master. Apart from this subjection of mind and body, there would be little development in Christian character.

Counting the Cost

The commitment expected in the church, thus, allowed for no reservations, no discharge from duty. One did not have to be smart or talented to enroll in Christ's mission, but one had to be faithful. The cross permitted no compromise. No mere mouthing of creeds here! Affirming that "Jesus is Lord" was a pledge of complete submission to His authority; all that they were, all that they had answered to His command; and their greatest joy was in beholding His glory.

Renouncing the old patterns of self-exaltation was the choice made in repentance. It meant a complete change of mind, turning around or converting "from darkness to light and from the power of Satan unto God" (26:18; cf. 11:21; 14:15; 15:19; 26:20; 28:27). As for known sin, the break with the past was complete. Even relics and books that carried connotations of the sinful past, like the magical scrolls at Ephesus, were destroyed (19:19; cf. 19:26). Paul would call this bringing forth "works worthy of repentance" (26:20). Sincerity may be questioned until there is such resolution. The demand, therefore, was unequivocable: "Repent ye therefore, and turn again, that your sins may be blotted out, that so there may come seasons of refreshing from the presence of the Lord" (3:19; cf. 5:31; 8:22; 11:18).

Baptism witnessed to the convert's new life in Christ (2:38, 41; 8:12, 36–38; 9:18; 10:47, 48; 16:15, 33; 18:8; 19:5; 22:16). As such, it was a sacramental sign of saving grace, indicating cleansing, rebirth, and passage into the Christian community (1 Cor. 6:11; 12:13; Titus 3:5; Rom. 6:3, 4). Though the external rite itself did not bestow spiritual life, it was a vivid identification with the claims of the Messiah-King, and where properly observed, a means by which the Spirit of God could bring great blessing to the soul. That one would submit to this ordinance, publicly indicating allegiance to Christ, was a bold verification of faith.[4]

This choice was costly and not to be entered into inadvisedly. To be sure, there were some who went through the forms of profession with no sense of commitment, as

---

4. In light of the personal choice, the question of infant baptism might be raised. It does not appear that Acts gives large support to the practice, although some will find allusion to it in the baptism of the households of Cornelius (10:44–48), Lydia (16:14, 15) and the Philippian jailer (16:33, 34). Probably more support can be claimed from the Hebrew custom of circumcising infants as a token of the Abrahamic covenant, if it is believed that baptism relates to circumcision. However baptism may be viewed, the New Testament teaches that salvation is a personal matter, and cannot be passed on through mere ceremonial observances (John 8:39–59). This necessity for the individual's consent finds expression in many churches today through the practice of confirmation.

with Simon Magus.[5] But for those who truly took their stand with Christ, when the decision was understood, it meant a reorientation of life. The things that this world holds dear no longer held the same appeal. To the devotees of Mammon, such a commitment seemed utterly foolish, but to those who were saved, the way of the cross was the wisdom and the power of God.

Continuing in the Way

The renewal of that decision in daily obedience proved the new Christian's determination. What was said of the converts at Pentecost could apply generally to the church: "They continued stedfastly" in the doctrine embraced (2:42; cf. 13:43; 14:22). Another description is so apropos to the Christian tenacity of purpose: they "cleave unto the Lord" (11:23; cf. 17:34). Peter expressed this quality well when he declared, come what may, "We must obey God rather than men" (5:29). Fully persuaded of the rightness of their cause, they would not be diverted from the Way set before them.

This faithfulness kept the disciples on course. When Jesus said to wait, they waited (1:4; 2:1). When the Scriptures were understood to mean that a replacement was needed for Judas, the 120 selected a twelfth man (1:15–26). When the apostles were told by an angel to go and speak the word of life, they went (5:19–21; cf. 8:27,

---

5. Simon had professed faith in Christ and been baptized by Philip (8:13), but he was still "in the gall of bitterness and in the bond of iniquity" (8:23). This example of the Scripture's own witness against insincerity in baptism is reason enough to avoid investing any outward ceremony with automatic divine favor. Unless the heart is right, the physical form is meaningless.

28). When Philip was commanded by the Spirit to join himself to the chariot of the eunuch, he "ran" (8:29, 30). When Peter in a vision received instructions to meet with the servants of the centurion, he "went down" to them (10:19–21; 11:12). When asked by the angel to leave the prison, he got up and "followed" him (12:7–10). When Paul was forbidden by the Spirit to travel in one direction, he moved in another (16:6–8). When the messenger from Macedonia besought him to come over and help them, "straightway" he made plans to go (16:10). Understandably, there were times when unity among them in respect to direction was not immediate, as when Paul felt he must go to Jerusalem. Knowing of the danger that awaited him there, a prophet, as well as some of his friends, counseled him against going (21:10–13). But when they saw that the apostle would not be dissuaded from the path set before him, the Christians agreed with his decision, saying, "the will of the Lord be done" (21:14).[6] This was the attitude typified throughout the Acts. When God's leading was clear, whatever it might entail, they were obedient.

The spiritual sensitivity it reflects can be seen also in the internal discipline of the church. Counsel of persons invested with authority was respected, as is evidenced in the way the congregation at Jerusalem responded to the

6. Some may feel that this was an instance in which Paul resisted guidance. However, a careful reading of the passage will indicate that the apostle was not told by the Spirit to avoid going to Jerusalem, but only of his mistreatment in the city. Later, when arrested, Paul was assured by the Lord that he was on the right course, and as he had been faithful in testifying in Jerusalem, so he "must" bear witness also at Rome (23:11). Assurance of God's will was given him again, this time by an angel, before the shipwreck on his voyage to stand before Caesar (27:23–25).

advice of the apostles, working out a solution to the murmuring of the Grecian widows (6:1-5). The adoption later of the actions in the general church council over the Gentile question shows the same attitude. When the consensus of the group was reached and the Spirit of God seemed pleased, the issue was settled (15:25-29). "The decrees to keep" which had been ordained of the apostles and elders at Jerusalem were then circulated across the church, apparently with acceptance, for "the churches were strengthened in the faith . . ." (16:4, 5). Perhaps the most beautiful example of this perceptivity to guidance is at Antioch. Told by the Spirit to separate Barnabas and Saul for the work to which they were called, the congregation obeyed and sent their two best men overseas as missionaries (13:2-4). Though the decision may have been difficult, they trusted God, knowing that His will was perfect.

Such faith in practice gave direction to the Christian community. Had it not been for their willingness to follow orders, even under hardship, one wonders how they could have survived the disorienting conditions in which they lived. They were always under pressure, facing the beguilements of an evil age. Yet through it all, they walked with confidence. There was a spring in their step, a sparkle in their eyes. They were led because they obeyed. That obedience, in turn, led them to learn more of Christ.

Authority of Scripture

Giving direction and stability to their walk was the Holy Scripture. The New Testament books were just beginning to be written during the period of Acts, but the inspired writings of the Old Covenant were always near at hand. The Judaistic Christians had heard them read and expounded in the synagogues every Sabbath as long as they could remember, and they implicitly believed them to be the oracles of God (1:16; 28:25; 13:34, 35; cf. 1 Pet. 1:25). In them was the promise of their Messiah Savior, which gave meaning and personal fulfillment to that which was written. As the Letters of the apostles became available, along with the Gospels, they were added to the sacred canon, and accorded the same respect (2 Tim. 3:16; 2 Pet. 1:21). Included in this deposit of unerring truth was the content of the apostolic message, focusing the whole Revelation of God's Word, written, spoken, and living in Christ.[7]

This Word sent from God permeated the life of the church (10:36; 13:26). The Words of the ancient patriarchs, kings, and prophets mingled with those of the apostles in a united witness to the Savior (e.g. 2:17–22; 7:42, 43; 13:29; 15:15–18; 24:14).[8] Here was the authority

---

7. Of the approximately fifty references to an inspired source of truth, the terms "Scripture," (γραφή), or "written," *graphe/grapho* (γράφω) appear fourteen times in Acts, with the remainder simply being the term "Word," *logos* (λόγος), separated by or in combination with qualifying terms, such as "the Word of God" or "the Word of the Lord." A term for speech, *rhema* (ῥῆμα), often translated "word," is also used a time or two referring to Scripture. To this might be added, "Gospel" and "promise." These various terms are used interchangeably and taken together disclose the fullness of God's Testament in Christ.

8. References to the Old Testament, either by direct quotation, synopsis of a passage, or allusion to some event, occur nearly 200 times in the Acts, mostly in the apostles' sermons. In some of the messages to the Jews, like Peter's proclamation at Pentecost or Stephen's defense before the Council, over half of the recorded sermon makes use of the Old Testament Scripture.

of their preaching (e.g. 8:4; 13:5; 15:35); teaching (e.g. 15:35; 18:11, 28); testimony (e.g. 14:3) and personal evangelism (e.g. 8:32, 35; 18:28). Nothing is ever said about their homiletical skills, impressive as they may have been. But again and again it is recorded that people received God's Word with gladness (2:41; 4:4; 8:14; 10:44; 11:1; 17:11). When the Gentiles at Antioch in Pisidia heard it, they actually "glorified the Word of God" (13:48). This was what hungry, contrite hearts yearn to hear—a divinely authenticated message of salvation (e.g. 13:7, 42, 44; 15:7; 19:10; 22:22). A gifted speaker, of course, may enhance the presentation, but it is not the communicator who saves. Nor can persons rest their faith upon any human experience, however sincere. Finally, it is the Word of the Gospel alone that can bring redemption to a believing soul (1 Pet. 1:23).

The importance placed upon this infallible source of truth in the church can be seen in the apostles' request that they be relieved from some housekeeping responsibilities in order to have more time for "the ministry of the word" (6:4). This was the area, along with prayer, where they supremely felt their own need. As they explained, ". . . It is not fit that we should forsake the word of God, and serve tables" (6:2). The people concurred, for they, too, recognized the priority of this spiritual discipline, not merely for the sake of the apostles' own development and outreach, but also, through their leadership, for the nurture of the church in ministry.

The Word of grace was the means by which the whole body was to be built up and given an "inheritance among all them that are sanctified" (20:32; cf. Eph. 5:26; 2 Tim. 2:21; John 15:3; 17:17). In this the Bereans set a good example, when we are told that they were "examining the

Scriptures daily," checking out what they heard with God's written authority (17:11; cf. 2 Tim. 2:15). Judging from the repetitious mention of the Word throughout the narrative, it would appear that the practice was quite widespread. The early Christians were constantly learning because they were earnestly seeking the direction of the Bible. This was their Guidebook for faith and life. It should not go unnoticed, too, that as "the word of God increased," so did "the number of the disciples" (6:7). Genuine church growth and growing in the Word go together (12:24; 19:20).

A Praying People

To this must be added prayer—the communion of the soul with the Spirit of the Lord. What God reveals through His Word invites spiritual communication with the Author of Scripture, creating an atmosphere of devotion in the obedient life. Such worship pulsates through the early church. Whether in private supplication or in their fellowship together, the Christians are a praying people. In fact, more mention is specifically made of prayer in Acts than in any other book of the New Testament.[9]

---

9. Altogether there are thirty-one references to prayer in the Book of Acts. Of these instances, the word *proseuchomai* (προσεύχομαι), "to pray" or "wish for," is used sixteen times; while the noun form *proseuche* (προσευχή), "a prayer" or "pour out," occurs nine times, two of these referring to a place of prayer. The word *deomai* (δέομαι), "to pray, request, want," is used seven times, but only five of these refer to a prayer to God. Two other words in Acts, "to ask" and "to call," which elsewhere in the New Testament may refer to divine entreaty, do not acquire this meaning in Acts. Once the word *densis* (δέησις), "supplication," is used, calling for particular benefits. Among the

Indicative of its centrality, out of a prayer meeting the church was born (1:14), and they continued unwaveringly in this communion (2:42; 6:4). They prayed when challenged by opposition and physical danger (4:24; 12:5; 16:25; 18:9, 10). They prayed when in need of divine guidance (1:24; 9:11; 22:17, 18). They prayed when burdened for others' spiritual needs (8:15; 19:6). They prayed when ministering to the sick and hopeless (9:40; 16:16; 28:8). They prayed when commissioning persons for special service (6:6; 13:3; 14:23). They prayed when parting (20:36; 21:5). They prayed when facing death (7:59, 60).

One cannot help but notice the varied locations and times of prayer. They observed the custom of praying in the temple, of course (3:1; 16:16). But more often prayer was noted in their homes (1:13, 14; 9:11; 12:12; 14:23), sometimes on the housetop (10:9). They prayed by the riverside (16:13); they prayed on the seashore (21:5); they prayed on shipboard (27:35); they prayed in jail (16:25). At the noon hour (10:9), in the afternoon (3:1); and even at midnight they prayed (16:25). They seemed to feel that God would hear a sincere prayer anywhere and anytime. Apparently the admonition of their Lord had not been dismissed when He said that men "ought always to pray, and not to faint" (Luke 18:1).

The association of prayer with the whole life-style of the church comes out clearly in the frequent use of the participle, a grammatical form that links its action with

---

other New Testament books, next in prominence to references to prayer is the Gospel of Luke, with thirty instances, indicating the significance with which it was regarded, both in the record of Christ and His church. The mere repetition of certain words may not be definitive, but it establishes an emphasis that cannot be ignored.

the leading verb. In this connection, prayer is related to regular periods of devotion (10:30), the gathering together of the church (12:12), seeking direction (1:24), visions (11:5), commissioning for service (6:6; 13:3; 14:23), inspirations (22:17), healing (28:8f), the mighty shaking of the earth (16:25), giving (10:2), and saying farewell (21:5). These constructions, and the tenses used, have the effect of weaving communion with the Spirit into everything happening.[10] Prayer is not some distant goal the church is striving to reach, but rather it is a present and continuing fact of their experience.

What may be the most remarkable aspect about their prayers is the way they are answered. In most cases the nature of the request is not stated, but when it can be determined from the text or the circumstances, God gave them what they asked for. There were unrecorded exceptions to this pattern, I am sure, and some instances are mentioned in other Books of the Bible, as was the case with Paul's request that he be delivered from his thorn in the flesh (2 Cor. 12:7–9); but in the story of Acts, prayer always seems to be right on the mark. A more convincing evidence of a church living largely in the will of God could hardly be imagined.

---

10. Of the twenty-one instances in which a verb form is used denoting prayer, twelve are participles, equally divided between the present tense, representing a continuing action or action simultaneous to the leading verb, and the aorist tense, indicating action antecedent to the leading verb or a simple event. The other nine verbs occur in the present indicative tense twice, denoting a continuing action and present action in progress; the aorist passive imperative twice, to express a command; and the aorist infinitive once, underscoring purpose. The ten other usages of words for prayer in Acts are nouns.

An Example of Prayer

An impression of how they prevailed with God may be gained from the prayer of the Jerusalem brethren when learning of the threats against Peter and John (4:23–31). Lifting up their voices to heaven, "with one accord" (v. 24), they affirmed the absolute sovereignty of their Lord, Creator of heaven and earth. The prayer speaks of God's revelation in Scripture, noting that His foreknowledge embraces all events, including the hostile attitude of kings and rulers toward Himself and His Anointed. The Lord of history is never caught by surprise. Nothing can happen without first passing through His will. This is supremely demonstrated in the treatment accorded His "holy servant Jesus," who fulfilled God's purpose at the cross. What appeared as defeat was actually victory. How wonderful in prayer to see all that takes place in the light of divine providence!

With the triumph of their Lord in view, the Christians interpreted their need of grace. Calling upon the Lord to look upon their problem, they said: ". . . Grant unto thy servants to speak thy word with all boldness, while thou stretchest forth thy hand to heal; and that signs and wonders may be done through the name of thy holy servant Jesus" (4:29, 30). Their concern was not that they be removed from adversity, but rather that in the face of persecution, they might continue their ministry to the praise of God. Here is the spirit of real prayer. When the glory of the Lord is our consuming desire, then we are on praying ground.

That God is pleased with such intercessions becomes immediately apparent, for "the place was shaken wherein they were gathered together"; they were filled with the

Holy Spirit, and with "boldness" they spoke the Word of God (4:31). As an added bonus, a beautiful sense of unity and compassion settled down upon the church, and ". . . great grace was upon them all" (4:33). When we pray in the will of God, it seems that He delights to give more blessing than we ask for or even imagine.

Periods of Fasting

Sometimes fasting was coupled with prayer. This voluntary discipline of abstinence from food was commonly practiced in Israel and had been observed by Jesus.[11] Though the custom must not become an end in itself or be relied on as a means of earning divine favor, as it did with the Pharisees, properly followed fasting permits one to have more time for prayer and reflection upon the things of God. When this purpose is clear, the discipline can help bring the body and mind into subjection to the Spirit, increasing sensitivity to nonmaterial reality.

It is given particular prominence in Acts when in prayer individuals and congregations were seeking special guidance of the Lord (9:9; 10:30; 13:2, 3; 14:23). Dur-

---

11. There is record that Jesus fasted for forty days before embarking on His public ministry (Matt. 4:1, 2; Mark 1:12, 13; Luke 4:2). Though this practice is not given much attention in the Gospels thereafter, apparently fasting and prayer was a part of His discipline (e.g. Mark 6:31, 46; John 4:31–34), and He urged it upon His disciples (Matt. 17:21; Mark 9:29). Whether or not He fasted twice a week, like the Pharisees, is not stated, although in pointing out the abuse of the custom, His language, "when ye fast," assumes that His disciples followed some kind of ritual (Matt. 6:16). That they did not have the works of austerity which typified the Pharisees, as well as the followers of John the Baptist (Mark 2:18), seems evident. However, Jesus assured them that fasting should be taken more seriously after He was gone (Mark 2:20).

ing times of trial and testing, also, fasting is noted (27:21, 33). Paul, in his letters, mentions his own fasting (2 Cor. 6:5; 11:27), obviously with personal profit, for he strongly commends the practice to the church (1 Cor. 7:5). We would do well to follow the admonition.

Rejoicing in Adversity

Foregoing food or pleasure for a spiritual purpose may have been easier for the apostolic Christians than for us, for they generally had less encumbrances or affluence to worry about. Yet what they had they freely shared with others (2:44, 45; 4:34–37; 11:29; 2 Cor. 8:1–4). Material possessions were held with an open hand.[12] They knew how to abound whether with much or with little (e.g. Phil. 4:12). What mattered to them was not the abundance of things possessed, but the way everything was received as a gift of God and returned to Him as an offering of thanksgiving (cf. 20:35; Heb. 13:15, 16).

Even their ill-treatment by the world was accepted in this spirit. When beaten, the apostles rejoiced "that they were counted worthy to suffer dishonor" for Jesus (5:41). In prison they were heard singing "hymns unto God"

12. Though the majority of the believers were probably poor, as most of the population, there were some among them who would be considered wealthy. Barnabas, for example, possessed land, as did others (4:34, 36, 37). Mary, the mother of John Mark, owned a house, and had a servant girl (12:12, 13). In fact, it is reasonable to assume that the church met in houses owned by the members. Cornelius, Lydia, Aquila and Priscilla, even Paul, to mention a few, were persons of means. It is not wealth that is evil, but the love of money. The rich and powerful may have more temptation to ignore the spiritual dimension of life, but materialism is a plague that can infect and destroy anyone, including the destitute.

(16:25). Arraigned before Agrippa on trial for his life, Paul was "happy" for another opportunity to give his testimony (26:2). When being stoned to death, Stephen, with a vision of his Lord in heaven, could only think to pray for his misguided murderers (7:60). What can you do with such people? Being reviled, they bless; being defamed, they entreat; being persecuted, they bear it as a badge of honor (1 Cor. 4:12, 13).

An insight to the Christian attitude comes out of the "Letter to Diognetus," possibly dating from the second century.

> They love all men and are persecuted by all. . . . They are dishonored, and yet have their glory in this very dishonor. They are insulted, and just in this they are vindicated. They are abused, and yet they bless. They are assaulted, and yet it is they who show respect. Doing good, they are sentenced like evildoers. When punished with death, they rejoice in the certainty of being awakened to life.[13]

Living as Martyrs

That the disciples could take the abuse of society without showing bitterness toward their tormentors goes back again to their commitment to follow Jesus. Since He had endured the cross for them, how could they complain about hardship in His ministry? ". . . A servant is not greater than his lord . . ." (John 15:20; cf. 15:18–25). So as

---

13. "Letter to Diognetus," in the compilation of Eberhard Arnold, *The Early Christians* (Grand Rapids, Mich.: Baker Book House, 1979), 109, 110.

with their Master, the disciples learned obedience through suffering (cf. Heb. 5:8). They were ostracized from family and friends (e.g. 5:13; 13:45; 18:6; 28:25). Threats from their antagonists were commonplace (e.g. 4:3, 21; 5:33; 17:13; 19:29, 30; 21:10, 11); plots to kill them were rife (9:23, 29; 14:5; 23:12, 13). Persecution forced many to flee from their homes for safety (8:1; 11:19). They were often arrested and thrown into prison (5:18; 12:3–5; 16:24; 23:35). Their leaders were flogged with many stripes (5:40; 16:22, 23; 22:24), bound with chains (21:33; 22:30), smitten in the face (23:2), and stoned by enraged mobs (7:58; 14:19).[14]

Paul's recounting of his sufferings expressed the sacrifice one should be willing to make for the Gospel. In addition to the physical torments and imprisonments, he was in constant journeyings, perils of the sea and wilderness, perils of robbers, perils of his own countrymen, perils of the heathen, perils among false brethren, "in labor and travail, in watchings often, in hunger and thirst, in fastings often, in cold and nakedness," and beside all this, he had the daily care of the churches (2 Cor. 11:24–28). Yet as he said, none of these hardships distracted him, for he was willing to suffer the loss of all things that he might know Christ and "the power of his resurrection, and the fellowship of his sufferings, becoming conformed unto his death" (Phil. 3:7–10).

---

14. An overall treatment of persecutions in the early church will be found in Thieleman J. Van, comp., *The Bloody Theater or Martyrs Mirror of Defenseless Christians* (Scottdale, Penn.: Herald Press, 1950), esp. 1–99. A less comprehensive account is in William Bryan Torbush, ed., *Foxe's Book of Martyrs* (Philadelphia: John C. Winston Co., 1926). A book by Herbert B. Workman, *Persecution in the Early Church* (London: Epworth Press, 1906) follows a more cautious approach.

That commitment made the Christians invincible. Having already faced the cross, they could look opposition in the eye, without flinching, knowing that they were "more than conquerors" through Christ (Rom. 8:37). It is significant that the word *witness*, which Jesus used in reference to the disciples (1:8), means "martyr," and is so translated several times in the New Testament (22:20; Rev. 2:13; 17:6).[15] Those who speak the Word must be willing to die for it (21:13). This was their martyrdom—a daily dying with Christ—that put a song in the heart of the church. Realizing they were dead, buried, and raised with Christ, what had they to fear? They belonged to Him who had defeated every enemy. So whether they lived or died, what difference did it make? They were "the Lord's" (Rom. 14:8).

Spiritual Warfare

In this confidence they went forth boldly to challenge "the power of Satan" (26:18). There was no illusion in the

---

15. The term *martus* (μάρτυς) originally simply had reference to one witnessing to the truth, but it came to include "those who seal the seriousness of their witness or confession by death." Gerhard Kittel, ed. *Theological Dictionary of the New Testament,* ed. and trans. Geoffrey W. Bromiley (Grand Rapids, Mich.: Wm. B. Eerdmans, 1967), 505. The distinction between *witness* and *martyr* begins to emerge in the second century, though as late as the fifth century the two are still used interchangeably. Augustine, about A.D. 416, commenting on the term *witness* in 1 John 1:2, wrote: "Christian lips utter this word daily, and would that the name were also in our hearts, so that we imitated the constancy of the martyrs in their sufferings. The martyrs were God's witnesses." Tract. in Ep., Jo. 1, 2, quoted in Jerome Aixala, *Witnessing and Martyrdom* (Bombay: St. Paul Publications, 1969), 92; *also* Robert E. Coleman, *The Mind of the Master* (Old Tappan, N.J.: Fleming H. Revell, 1977), 100–101.

mind of the church about her enemy. The struggle in the world was not with "flesh and blood," but against mighty forces of evil (26:18), "powers" and "principalities," rulers of darkness in high places (Eph. 6:12). All the legions of hell were arrayed against the servants of God, and they knew full well that the devil would seek to defeat, or at least nullify the work of God (13:10; cf. John 13:2; 2 Cor. 4:4; 1 Pet. 5:8).

Many churchmen today seem oblivious to this satanic conspiracy. It is like caring for casualties on a battlefield without ever trying to stop the instigator of the carnage. Beelzebub is quite accommodating to such naiveté. He will allow almost any program to go on, even the appearance of church growth, as long as it does not interfere with his control. By avoiding conflict with the adversary, things may move along contentedly for a while, but in the end there will be destruction.

The church must recognize that we are in spiritual warfare. Anyone not willing to live under orders and endure hardships as a soldier of Christ will be no match for the enemy.[16] This is a battle unto death. We must come under strict discipline of body, mind, and spirit. There is no place in this service for the double-minded or the sluggard. Only those who are crucified with Christ will know the victory that overcomes the world.

The Application Today

We dare not obscure the altar of sacrifice, where consecration to God is complete. If we try to circumvent the

---

16. Adolf Harnack notes that a name given to early Christians was "a soldier of Christ," *The Mission and Expansion of Christianity in the First Three Centuries,* trans. and ed. James Moffatt (New York: Williams & Norgate, 1908), 414.

cross, we assure our own ultimate defeat, for we cut the nerve of obedience and kill the life-style of the Great Commission. No one will take seriously the command to make disciples who has not taken up the cross.

Strangely, today we hear little about self-denial and suffering in all the talk about church growth. Is this because most of what has been said to date has come out of the Western world, where affluence abounds and church affiliation is a mark of social acceptance, if not good politics? Unwittingly, I am afraid, Christian discipleship has often been squeezed into this world's mold, so that prosperity and success are more cherished than radical obedience. But it will not stand the test of time. When the standards of church membership are set by popular demand, eventually the church becomes so much like the world that there is no reason for the world to change. The very effort of the church to appease fleshly expectations makes her unattractive.

Already this may be happening. The church as a whole in North American is barely keeping pace with the increase in population. In Western Europe there is steady decline. To see significant growth, more likely than not we will need to go beyond the easy-going, self-indulgent religious life of the West. It is the church living under oppression and poverty, usually in underdeveloped countries of the world, where the most thrilling growth is happening today. I am not suggesting that all of these non-Western lands have vibrant churches, anymore than all congregations in the West lack vitality, but a general pattern can be observed. It is interesting, too, that for the most part the people in these growing segments of the Third World Christian community have had little, if any, opportunity to receive extensive formal training or even attend a church-growth seminar. Obviously sophisticated theological education, with all its assumed expertise in churchmanship, does not produce the life-style of Jesus.

Have the opulence and freedoms of the Western world, though wrought with great potential for good, lulled a complacent church into mediocrity? If that is the case, any circumstance that removes these artificial supports from us should be seen as an act of mercy. Our Lord is more interested in developing our character than in preserving our comfort. Whatever it takes, we must get back to basic Christianity, align our wills with the way God has set for us, and move out to disciple the nations. In many instances, church membership standards must be raised, reflecting higher expectations of commitment and disciplined living. The congregation may be slow to understand, but those in positions of authority can lead the way for others to follow and show by their example what it means to be true witnesses of Christ.

Yet obedience alone can become brittle and weary in well-doing. There must be an inner dynamic motivating and empowering life with love, an actual partaking of the divine nature. To bring this truth into focus, one final principle must be stressed, apart from which everything else written thus far would be sounding brass and tinkling cymbal.

6

The Power to Become

Enabling Power

Jesus knew that His work on earth could never be done by human striving, however determined the effort. Power to be His witnesses could only come through the Spirit of God (1:8). So before He left the disciples, He told them to wait for "the promise of the Father," for they would "be baptized in the Holy Spirit not many days hence" (1:4, 5). In fact, they were instructed not to leave Jerusalem until they had received this promised heavenly enduement

(Luke 24:49). Anticipating the outpouring, even as He authorized their mission, Jesus breathed on the disciples, and said, "Receive ye the Holy Spirit" (John 20:22).

Clearly the power for witnessing was not in themselves, but in the Eternal Spirit, the enabling Agent of the Kingdom, communicating and effecting the will of God.[1] By His creative power the worlds were made and the stars hung in place (Gen. 1:2). The Spirit fashioned man in the divine image, then breathed upon him, and he became a living soul (Gen. 2:7; Job 33:4). When the creature turned to his own way, it was this same Spirit who sought to bring the rebel back and effect reconciliation with God. All through the Old Testament He can be seen at work with chosen people, at special times and places, making a nation to be His witness in a fallen world (Isa. 43:10; 44:8; 49:6). Though the Spirit's power only rested upon a few people in the unfolding drama of salvation, a day was envisioned when He would come upon One in absolute and permanent majesty (Isa. 11:1, 2; 32:18), and through that One the Kingdom age would dawn and the mighty power of the Most High would be poured forth upon all flesh (Isa. 32:15; cf. Joel 2:28–32).

In the fullness of time the creating Person of the Trinity planted the seed of the Father in the womb of the virgin, so that she conceived and gave birth to the only begotten Son of God (Matt. 1:18, 20; Luke 1:35). Thereafter, the Spirit directed Jesus during the days of His incarnate life (Luke 4:1, 14). Everything He said and did was in cooper-

---

1. For a brief review of this agelong ministry of the Spirit, along with bibliographic sources for further study, *see* Robert E. Coleman, *The Mind of the Master* (Old Tappan, N.J.: Fleming H. Revell, 1977), 21–36.

ation with the Holy Spirit. He anointed Him to preach
and to heal (10:38; Luke 4:18, 19). He empowered Him to
cast out demons (Matt. 12:28). He sustained Him in suffering. At last, He brought the Son to offer Himself up as
a sacrifice for the sins of the world (Heb. 9:14); then, in
death-rending triumph, He raised Him from the grave
(Rom. 8:11). Make no mistake, God's work, whatever the
form, is accomplished only through the Holy Spirit.

Another Comforter

Yet this power is not some vague, impersonal energy in
the universe. The Spirit is a Person, the Third Member of
the Holy Trinity, with the same quality of character revealed in the Son. This was beautifully explained by
Jesus to the disciples shortly before He was taken away
and crucified. As they were together in the Upper Room,
following the Last Supper, He told them that He would
soon return to heaven, but that He would not leave them
orphans. For He would ask the Father to send them "another Comforter, . . . even the Spirit of truth" (John 14:16,
17; 16:7). The reference was to a Person like Himself, One
who would stand by their side, "Another" who would
take the same place with them, in the unseen realm of reality that Christ had filled in the visible experience of life.
There was but one difference. Whereas Jesus in the flesh
was limited to His earthly body, now this physical barrier
would no longer exist, and by His Spirit the disciples
could live continually in His fellowship. This was no
makeshift substitute, but the promise of the real Presence
of their Lord.

Just as Jesus had led them when they were together, now the Spirit would guide them into truth (John 16:13). He would teach them what they needed to learn (John 14:26). He would help them pray (John 14:12, 13; 16:23, 24). He would give them utterance to speak (Matt. 10:19, 20; Mark 13:11; Luke 12:12), and by His strength, they would do the very works of Christ, and even "greater works than these" (John 14:12).

Through it all, the Spirit would glorify the Son (John 16:14). That supremely is His ministry—to take the things of Christ and show them unto His people (John 16:15). The world could not receive this teaching, for it did not know Jesus; but the disciples knew Him, for He was with them, and in His Spirit, He would abide in their midst forever (John 14:17).

Of course, the Spirit had already been with them in their association with the Savior, but in a more wonderful way, He was now to glorify Christ in and through their witness. Until Jesus had finished His work on earth and was exalted at the right hand of God (John 7:39), this could not be realized. Only after He assumed His kingly reign on the throne could the Spirit be released in power upon the church, not for a few years, but for an age; not on a few select individuals, but on all who would receive Him.

In this manifestation the Great Commission would be fulfilled. Having given His disciples the command to disciple the nations, Jesus assured them: "... Lo, I am with you always, even unto the end of the world" (Matt. 28:20). It was not a promise to be realized when they got to heaven, but a present blessing experienced in the process of making disciples. Mandating this ministry, Christ was simply asking that His church continue in His fellowship by working with Him in reaching the world.

We can understand why He charged the disciples to tarry until they be endued with power. How else could they ever do His work? The exalted Christ needed to become a living reality in their lives. The Enabler of His Kingdom mission had to fully possess them, purifying their hearts and directing their thoughts. Unless they were enthralled by His Presence, the work of their Lord would never thrill their souls. Nothing less than a personal baptism of fire, an enduement of power from on High, would suffice for the task at hand.

The Pentecostal Outpouring

The promise began to be fulfilled at Pentecost. As the disciples were assembled in the Upper Room, "suddenly there came from heaven a sound as of the rushing of a mighty wind, and it filled all the house where they were sitting" (2:2). The wind,[2] symbolizing the strength of the Spirit, came first to the house of God, from whence it would sweep across the earth with life-giving power. Then "there appeared unto them tongues parting asunder, like as of fire," a flame resting on the head of each person. The distribution of the sacred fire pointed to the

---

2. In the Hebrew language the words *spirit* and *wind* or *breath* are identical. So the sound of rushing wind would have immediately awakened in the Jewish hearers expectations of the Spirit of God (cf. John 3:8; 6:18; Matt. 7:25, 27; Luke 12:55). A perusal of a good Greek word dictionary is very rewarding, such as Colin Brown, *The New International Dictionary of New Testament Theology*, vol. 3 (Grand Rapids, Mich.: Regency Reference Lib., Zondervan, 1976), 689–709.

truth that the Spirit had come to dwell, not with a few officers of the society, but with all the members of the church, and everyone would minister in the manner to which they were called (2:3). Descriptive, too, of their witness-bearing appointment, they "began to speak with other tongues, as the Spirit gave them utterance" (2:4), going out among the people declaring what God had done (2:5–13).

The enduring miracle, however, was not in the outward phenomena associated with the initial outpouring, but in the inward realization of the exalted Christ which came to those "filled with the Holy Spirit" (2:4). To the church it was proof that Jesus was reigning in heaven. ". . . Having received of the Father the promise of the Holy Spirit," Peter explained, "He hath poured forth this . . ." (2:33). Pentecost was the culminating act in an agelong process of redemptive activity, the final step in the descent of the divine into the human. Jesus as an external Presence now became the enthroned Sovereign in the hearts of His people. A new era of the Kingdom had begun in Spirit-endued witnesses. The Gospel had become life and power within them. At last they were ready to go forth as laborers in the harvest of the Lord.

This fruit-bearing ministry of the church was beautifully symbolized in the Jewish Feast of Pentecost. On this day for hundreds of years the firstfruits of the grain harvest had been brought to the temple as a thank offering to God. For the Christians, though, it marked the firstfruits of a different kind of harvest, the first day of a great gathering of converts into the church. As such, it was the beginning of an age of evangelism that would not end until the children of the New Covenant were called out from every tongue and tribe and nation.

Acts of the Spirit

The full significance of what Pentecost meant becomes increasingly apparent as the story unfolds. With obvious intent, the whole early church movement is attributed to the Spirit's activity. Over fifty times He is specifically mentioned, more than in any other book of the Bible. So prominent is the Spirit in the narrative that the book has been properly called "The Acts of the Holy Spirit."

It is by His power that the disciples witness for Christ with boldness (1:8; 2:4; 4:8, 31; 5:32; 6:10; 13:9; 19:6), and through His enablement, persons were equipped for ministry (2:17, 18; 4:8; 6:3, 5; 9:17; 11:28; 19:6; 20:28; 21:4, 11). Joy and comfort in the Spirit come to faithful servants of the Lord (7:55; 8:39; 9:31; 11:24; 13:52; 20:23). He gives direction through the inspired Scripture (1:2, 16; 28:25), and Spirit-filled persons sensitive to His voice receive special guidance in crucial situations (8:29, 39; 10:19; 11:12, 28; 13:2, 4; 16:6, 7; 21:4, 11). Not only does He help in making decisions, the Spirit confirms truth to the hearts of the brethren (5:32; 15:8, 28). His leadership role is noted in matters of Church discipline and administration (5:3, 9; 6:3, 5; 7:51; 15:28; 20:28). Prominence is given to the Spirit in the breakthrough of the Gospel to the Samaritans (8:15, 17, 18, 19) and the Gentiles at Caesarea (10:19, 44, 45, 47; 11:12, 15, 16; 15:8). He is instrumental in sending out the first missionaries at Antioch (13:2, 4) and assists in various ways, all through the expansion of the church, to the uttermost parts of the earth (13:9, 52; 16:6, 7; 19:2, 6; 20:23, 28; 21:4; 28:25).

Unmistakenly, the amazing multiplication of the apostolic witness was in the power and demonstration of the Holy Spirit. Being an account of acts, it could be no other way. Whenever God acts in power to accomplish His purposes, the divine Paraclete does the work.

Personal Experience

The action centers, not on dynamic programs or campaigns, but on persons prepared by the Spirit for the Master's use. Descriptions of the modes of enduement are variable and often interrelated. Sometimes the Spirit is depicted as a gift or described as "given" (2:38; 5:32; 8:18; 10:45; 11:16, 17; 15:8); at other times He is received (2:33, 38; 8:15, 17, 19; 10:47; 19:2). The terms look to the divine source of this graceful impartation and the realization of the promise in experience. Intertwined with these expressions, the Spirit is represented as being poured out, falling and coming upon people (2:17, 18, 33; 8:16; 10:44, 45; 11:15; 19:6). Also used is the ceremonial idea of baptizing, which identifies the experience of those concerned with the message of John and the teachings of Jesus (1:5; 11:16), while anointing of the Spirit relates to power to accomplish an appointed task (4:27; 10:38).

Most characteristic of the Acts is the designation "full" or "filled" with the Spirit. Used ten times, in a variety of situations, the figure conveys the idea of one's personality being entirely pervaded by the Spirit's power and influence (2:4; 4:8, 31; 6:3, 5; 7:55; 9:17; 11:24; 13:9, 52).[3] The force of the text is upon a quality of experience.[4] In some

---

3. Elsewhere in the New Testament the term is used in Luke 1:15, 41, 67; 4:1 and Eph 5:18. With the exception of the last reference, all the expressions occur in Luke's writing, which indicates that it was a favorite of his.

4. Of the ten occasions where the infilling is mentioned in Acts, never is the definite article used, which in the light of each context could not imply indefiniteness, so must relate to a quality or condition.

instances the words underscore an act of being filled; in other usages the emphasis is upon acting in the fullness of the Spirit. But always the scientific-minded Luke underscores the fact, both as an event and as a life. Without becoming embroiled in academic speculation, the expression simply bears testimony to a real situation—a disciple possessed by the Spirit of Christ.

This was the norm of Christian experience in the New Testament. Not that believers all lived in the reality, but it was everyone's privilege. Where members of the church were not abiding in the promise, they were exhorted to do so. Using strong drink as an example of how a person can come under the domination of another power, Paul conversely applies the principle to the Christians: "Be not drunken with wine, wherein is riot, but be filled with the Spirit" (Eph. 5:18).

Judging from this command, just because persons believe in Christ does not mean that they are filled with the Spirit. The experience of the Samaritans and Ephesians, if it can be equated with an infilling, would lead to a similar conclusion (8:12–18; 19:1–7). Yet no one can truly belong to Christ without having the Spirit (Rom. 8:9), which would indicate that receiving the Spirit in conversion is not necessarily synonymous with being filled.[5] This is something, however, which the writer of Acts does

---

5. Perhaps it would be fair to say that potentially everyone receives the Spirit's fullness upon receiving Christ, though the appropriation of the provision may not be realized. Where this mode is specifically mentioned in the Scripture, it would seem that the persons filled were already believers. This clarity does not pertain to the usage of "giving" and "receiving" the Spirit, though these terms are used in reference to the experience of the Caesareans, which Peter later associates with the outpouring at Pentecost (10:44–48; cf. 15:8, 9).

not take time to discuss. What matters to him is not the terminology or any implied theological position, but the reality of the Pentecostal experience itself and how it impacts life.

Meeting the Conditions

Attention centers upon persons acting in such submission to the claims of Christ that their lives are permeated by His Presence (5:32; cf. 1 Pet. 1:22). If there is resistance to His Way, of course, the flow of the Spirit is hindered, and frustration and defeat result. Pride, that residue of an uncrucified self, especially causes conflict. But whatever it is, whether a deed or disposition, when the Spirit brings awareness of wrongdoing, the sin must be confessed, and the contrite will aligned with Christ. Where the surrender is up-to-date, every believer can abide in the fullness of His Spirit.

This resignation to the will of God comes through in the circumstances preceding the infilling of the Spirit at Pentecost (1:4–2:1). Those persons gathered were resolved to wait for the promise as their Lord had commanded.[6] Not only did they continue in prayer, but they endeavored to fulfill every condition of the Scriptures they understood, even to the detail of selecting a person to take the place of the traitor. Some have felt that a replacement was not that important, or at least there was no need of haste. But the point is that the disciples were unwilling to leave any stone unturned that they believed necessary as

---

6. The waiting period was necessary in order that the Spirit's coming would coincide with the day of Pentecost. Thereafter there was no need to wait, as is borne out in the subsequent accounts of infilling. The only delay in being filled now would be due to an unwillingness on our part to meet the conditions.

a preparation for the Spirit's outpouring. They wanted their lives to be completely in harmony with the Word of God. I suspect, too, that during this ten-day period there was confession and apologizing among members of the group respecting the way some had acted following their Lord's arrest, not the least being Peter's shameful denial while Jesus was on trial. Whatever their interpersonal situation, if there were any resentments or ill feelings among them, they got it all straightened out, for the account makes clear that they came to be "in one accord" (1:14; 2:1).

Again this condition of yieldedness to God is illustrated in the prayer of the Christians at Jerusalem, following the imprisonment of Peter and John (4:24–30). With resignation to the foreordained "counsel" of their Lord, they lay themselves at His disposal, and are "filled with the Holy Spirit" (4:28, 31). The three days without sight in Paul's experience at Damascus afforded another period of heart-searching preparation for the filling of the Spirit (9:9, 11, 17). Doubtless during this time of prayer and fasting the new apostle had ample opportunity to bring himself in complete submission to his Lord.

Significantly in all these accounts prayer has an important role. For it is not only the admission of human weakness and the avenue through which the will is surrendered; prayer is the means by which faith lays hold upon the promises. That is what brings the blessing. Confession and consecration only prepare the heart to receive the gift of God. The victorious life in the Spirit comes when we actually trust ourselves into the possession of Him who gave Himself for us. Committing all to Him, we quit striving and simply rest upon His Word, much as one would lay an offering upon an altar.

In the final analysis, the filling of the Spirit, like any

other benefit of salvation, is all of grace. We do not have
to beg God for the Gift. The Comforter has already come.
Indeed, He is in the Christian. Our part is to give Him
control of our empty vessel. The Father delights to "give
the Holy Spirit to them that ask him" (Luke 11:13), and if
we "ask anything according to his will," we know that He
will grant the petition (1 John 5:14, 15).

The Spirit-filled life is the life of faith—a faith that
lives in obedience to the Word of God. That the disciples
would stay in the Upper Room, even after nine days had
passed, for no other reason than that their Master had
told them to tarry until the power came, is testimony to
their confidence. They believed that what their Lord said
He would do. It was noted later that Stephen was "a man
full of faith and of the Holy Spirit" (6:5). Likewise Barnabas was "full of the Holy Spirit and of faith" (11:24).
What was said of these Christians would characterize
every truly consecrated believer. The Spirit fills anyone
willing to trust everything to Jesus.

Living Holiness

In receiving the Spirit one partakes of the holiness of
God. Christians are thus appropriately called "saints" or
"holy ones," for that is the nature of their Lord (9:13, 32,
41; 26:10; Rom. 1:7; 1 Cor. 1:2; 2 Cor. 1:1; Eph. 1:1; Phil.
1:1; and more).[7] The term comes from a root meaning "to

---

7. Altogether believers are called "saints" about 55 times in the
New Testament, even when still carnal (e.g. 1 Cor. 6:2; 14:33; 16:1,
15). The degree of godliness in the Christian life does not determine
sainthood, but rather the state to which the believer has been intro-
duced by grace. It is expected, however, that such persons will develop in the life of holiness.

set apart," which in its moral reference, takes on the idea of separation from the profane. A saint is a person set apart from the world and owned entirely by God.

Such sainthood comes in conversion, when, through the Holy Spirit, one receives new life in Christ and sanctification begins (26:18). The experience of holiness grows as the obedient disciple learns more of "the word of his grace," which builds up faith and makes known the rightful inheritance of those who are set apart for God (20:32). As aspects of life are seen to be unholy, they must be brought into conformity with the character of the indwelling Spirit. This involves confrontation of that pesky disposition of self-centeredness, still asserting its own way; when recognized, it must be nailed to the cross. Never should a follower of the Lamb permit disobedience to continue. For "they that are of Christ Jesus have crucified the flesh with the passions and the lusts thereof" (Gal. 5:24) and reckon themselves "to be dead unto sin, but alive unto God" (Rom. 6:11).

In practical ethics, the holiness of the apostolic church is displayed in the integrity of their life. Honesty marked their business dealings. They did "not live according to the flesh."[8] It was obvious to all. Theophilus of Antioch, writing in the second century, noted:

> They practice continence, observe monogamy, guard chastity, and wipe out injustice, destroying sin with its root. With them justice is lived out, laws are kept, and faith is witnessed to by deeds.... They consider truth supreme. Grace protects them. Peace shields them. The

---

8. "Letter to Diognetus," comp. Eberhard Arnold, *The Early Christians* (Grand Rapids, Mich.: Baker Book House, 1979), 109.

> Holy Word leads them. Wisdom teaches them.
> Life is decisive. God is their King.[9]

Though worldlings felt reproved by the Christians' moral behavior, they had to admit that their word was true and their character beyond reproach.

Personal holiness found horizontal expression in concern for people. Athenagoros, one of the early church leaders, wrote that "the full measure of justice" to them was "found in rightly loving ourselves and our neighbors."[10] No wonder their pagan contemporaries were bewildered. "Look, how they love each other," they said. "See, how ready they are to die for one another."[11]

No longer preoccupied with their own selfishness, they entered wholeheartedly into the redemptive ministry of their Lord. Calvary love was infused in their hearts by the Holy Spirit. With this inward motivation, the Christians could not keep silent about the Gospel or ignore sorrowing humanity about them. Holiness constrained them to reach out in compassion for a dying world. As Paul said, he was "pure from the blood of all" people in that he had not shunned to declare unto them "the whole counsel of God" (20:26, 27; cf. 15:9; 18:6; James 1:27). Where sainthood has this apostolic ingredient, the life-style of the Great Commission becomes a burning compulsion, just as it was with Jesus.[12]

---

9. Theophilus of Antioch, "To Autolycus," ibid., 120, 121.

10. Athenagoros, "A Plea Regarding Christians," ibid., 118.

11. Recorded in the "Apology" of Tertullian, ibid., 112.

12. This is brought out forcefully by Jesus in His high priestly prayer, when He speaks of His own sanctification. It was not that He needed cleansing or empowering, but that He willingly and continually gave Himself to those He loved in order that they "might be sanctified through the truth." In time, as their sanctification found

If this dimension of sanctification is neglected, as is so often the case, cleansing from sin and empowerment for victorious living would seem to revolve around a selfish purpose and thereby repudiate the very thing from which we are delivered. The Spirit's work within the heart is not to gratify the desire for personal blessing, but to make us useful to Christ and to prepare us "unto every good work" (2 Tim. 2:21). Jesus said, "When the Holy Spirit is come upon you," then "ye shall be my witnesses" (1:8). We dare not take that which God has redeemed for His glory and divert it to our own ends. Such perversion, whatever the occasion, is most deadly when concealed under a guise of piety.

Judgment Upon Pretense

The fearsome judgment of God upon pretense is brought out early in the story of Acts. Following the account of the rapidly growing Jerusalem church and the magnanimous way that the multitude of believers were caring for one another's needs (4:31-37), the story is told of Ananias and Sapphira (5:1-11). This couple had sold a possession to give the amount to the church benevolent fund. When the payment was received, however, they decided to hold back part of the money for their own use. This would have been quite all right—believers were never required to donate all their resources to the church. But this couple pretended to give all they had. That was the sin—the conspiracy to deceive, which was an affront

---

expression in a Great Commission life-style, ultimately, through reproduction, the world would come to believe on Him (John 17:19, 20).

to the integrity of God. Under the beguiling suggestion of Satan, they lied to the Holy Spirit (5:3, 4, 9).

These church members were hypocrites. Perhaps at one time they were sincere in their profession, but the cost of maintaining a spirit of self-denial was too much for them. Whether it was an unsurrendered ambition or desire for religious recognition that prompted their action is not explained. But whatever the inducement, the withholding of the full price reflected an intent to glorify self rather than bring glory to their Lord.

God will not tolerate sacrilege, for it subverts His whole purpose of redemption to make a holy people. More than that, it brings duplicity and treachery into the church, which will invariably compromise the mission of Christ to reach the world with His Gospel. Had the sin of hypocrisy been allowed to go unchallenged, the whole thrust of making disciples would have been lost. Knowing what was at stake, the Spirit-filled Peter boldly confronted Ananias and Sapphira with their sin. The disclosure was so shattering that both pretenders instantly died and were taken out and buried by young men of the congregation.

The impact this incident had upon the people is not difficult to imagine. "Great fear came upon the whole church . . ." (5:11). It was a holy fear of sin, a godly reverence in the Presence of Him who is of purer eyes than to behold evil (Hab. 1:13). They knew that the church could not trifle with the holiness of God (5:12). Outside the church, the effect was no less profound, for fear came upon "all that heard" (5:5, 11). The sobering awareness of judgment upon pretense certainly caused people to think a second time before coming into the church fellowship just because of their loving care, and many were scared away (5:13). Yet, notwithstanding the severity of the holiness standard, "people magnified" the Christians (5:13), and believers were added to the Lord as never before (5:14). Persons tired of the masquerade of the world's vain pleasure are drawn to the beauty of true holiness.

No effort is made in the account of the New Testament church to conceal the shortcomings of persons identified as believers, and this is apparent in Acts. But also clear is the forthright manner misguided or reprobate persons are reproved and warned of impending judgment (8:18–24; cf. 1 Tim. 1:20; 2 Tim. 4:10, 14, 15; 1 John 2:19; Rev. 2:1–7, 12–29; 3:1–6, 14–22). Nothing hinders more the effective witness of the church than inconsistency in the lives of her members. Where it is observed, leadership must take action to deal with the offenders.[13] If the people of God are to fulfill their role in world evangelization, our way of life must reflect the Gospel we represent.

Christ-likeness Demonstrated

The demonstration of holiness has always been at the heart of God's strategy of world evangelization. To this end Israel was chosen to be His witness among the na-

---

13. The biblical pattern in enforcing standards is very plain. First the offender is to be approached in love privately and an effort made to resolve the issue. If the party at fault will not heed the admonition, then one or two more concerned friends are to go with the leader in another attempt to effect reconciliation, "that at the mouth of two witnesses or three every word may be established." If the person still refuses to repent, the matter should be brought before the church, and appropriate discipline rendered (Matt. 18:15–17; cf. 1 Cor. 5:5; 2 Cor. 13:2; Titus 3:10).

tions, that people beholding their holy manner of life
would want to follow their God. When the Jews suc-
cumbed to the sensate culture about them, God sent His
Son to raise up a new Israel, of which His life was witness.
The Spirit now is fashioning the church in that likeness in
order to show His glory to the ends of the earth.

The manifestation of this holiness made the ministry of
the church convincing. To a remarkable degree, one
could not help but see that the Christians were a different
breed. Precept and example blended together in authentic
witness. There was a strangeness about their manner of
life that created a mystery. They had a graciousness in
their manner of speech, yet a boldness in their testimony.
Obedience was joyful. Compassion seemed to overflow
from their fellowship. A purity of motive was evident in
their helpfulness. Obviously this was not a trait learned
from the world. Although they were commonly regarded
as uneducated and ignorant, still by looking at their life-
style, even their oppressors could tell that "they had been
with Jesus" (4:13). The print of His character was upon
them.

This became most obvious in their sufferings. They did
not let the bitterness and hostility of their enemies keep
them from loving. Though ill-treated, they lived above
the enmity of their society. Look at Stephen's testimony
to his antagonists and his subsequent stoning. Paul never
got over that sight or Stephen's Christ-like prayer in
death (7:58–60; 26:10; 1 Tim. 1:13). As with this saint,
truly the blood of the martyrs became their ultimate witness. What was seen in the life-style of James is another
graphic illustration, when according to tradition, the officer who guarded him in prison was so impressed by his

demeanor that he embraced his Savior and was beheaded with the apostle (12:2).[14]

The likeness of Christ in the disciples was the incontrovertible testimony to the Holy Spirit's dominance in their lives. Jesus had said that the Comforter would glorify Him, and that is exactly what is seen in Acts. References to the Person of Christ saturate the book.[15] One gets the impression that Jesus is actively present and personally continuing His work through the disciples. Is this not what He said He would do? The Spirit is simply demonstrating that Christ lives in His church.

The Application Today

Living in the fullness of the Holy Spirit is as much the privilege of Christians today as it was of those first disciples. Nothing about the "power from on high" is restricted to the apostolic church. "For to you is the promise, and to your children, and to all that are afar off" (2:39).

The guarantee is the power to become what God has called us to be. It is not a doctrine to cherish, but a reality to experience. To the degree that we take His Word to heart and make Christ Lord of our lives, we can expect to

14. Eusebius reports this in his *Ecclesiastical History* 11:2, as taken from Clement of Alexandria's seventh book of Hypotyposes, referred to by F. F. Bruce, *Commentary on the Book of Acts,* 248.

15. In addition to Jesus as Lord, He is called Prince, Savior, Son of Man, Son of God, Man, Voice, Way, Judge, Prophet, and Angel. Altogether He is identified by proper titles and pronouns nearly 300 times. Also He is ascribed active ministries, such as reigning, forgiving, adding to the church, speaking, guiding, delivering, opening hearts, working miracles, convicting, judging, giving, and bringing salvation.

do His work. Here is where the issue rests. For the Spirit will use any life that is surrendered to the Savior. It remains for us only to remove every known barrier in His way and by faith receive the promise. Though our vessel be small, still He will fill to capacity what we offer Him.

Better still, we can experience increasingly more of His holiness as we grow in understanding of Christ and ourselves. There is always more beyond. The freshness of His Presence is new every morning. Special anointings will be needed as work demands require greater sensitivity and strength. Yet we can be confident that, however difficult the task to which we are called, the Spirit is ever present to help, and His grace is all-sufficient.

In time we transmit what we are to those about us. The closer the association, the more powerful our witness becomes in shaping the lives of others, either for good or ill. What a staggering responsibility! Whether or not we like it, the very fact that we live in such a society calls us to a life of sainthood. Any compromise in our dedication to Christ invariably has adverse repercussions upon others. By the same criterion, we have in our fellowship the awesome opportunity to give an exemplary testimony to the transforming power of the Gospel.

Persons near us will come to know our failings and weaknesses, of course. But let them also see the readiness with which confession is made when we become aware of our sin. From the brokenness of heart occasioned by the knowledge of dishonoring God and the sincerity with which we seek to make amends for the error of our ways, observing people will learn that Christ-likeness is the supreme quest of our life. The fact that all of us come woefully short of the perfection of our Lord need be no refutation to our witness, if there is a transparent commitment to walk as best we can in the steps of Jesus.

We can lead even in our weakness when it is clear that a pure motive governs our actions and that, despite our shortcomings, we love the Lord our God with all our hearts, all our souls, all our minds, and that we love our neighbor as ourselves. In this devotion everything written in the law and the prophets finds fulfillment (Matt. 22:37–40). This is holiness as can be experienced by every child of grace. It is the bond by which the whole church can live in perfect harmony (Col. 3:14).

How desperately the world needs this demonstration today—the undaunted witness of holy love in the lifestyle of men and women filled with the Spirit of Christ. To this character other qualities can be added, but without it everything else lacks the ring of truth. God is making a people in His own image, a kingdom of priests who will serve Him forever. Those who have entered this reign participate in His program to make disciples of all nations. He is our Way. He is our Truth. He is our Life. In the measure that we partake of His Spirit we shall fulfill His destiny for the church.

Afterword

Living Purposefully

Writing to the church at Ephesus, Paul said: ". . . Live purposefully and worthily and accurately . . . making the very most of the time—buying up each opportunity—because the days are evil" (Eph. 5:15, 16 AMP). The admonition is no less appropriate for us, especially in view of the commission of Christ to disciple the nations.

Our Lord's command is a summons to live with the same sense of purpose that directed His steps. He has given us in His life-style a personal example of what the mandate involves, while the Acts of the Apostles relates that pattern in His church. Though the principles must be clothed with relevant applications in our contemporary situation, they offer us some guidelines to follow. If they are true, then we are obligated to implement them. When we move from ideas to action, the rubber meets the road.

Finding ways to put the concepts into practice, however, will not be easy. Christians, like other people, tend to get into ruts that meander with the path of least resistance. The exacting work of making disciples may require not only renewed dedication, but also a reorientation of our philosophy of ministry; and some persons, content with the status quo, will not understand, saying that they have never done it this way before. Change will come slowly and not without struggle. Spiritual formation in the church is much like raising a family: Bringing children to maturity takes a lot of patience on the part of the parents, as well as some good plans for training. Not everything believed beneficial will work. There is one thing about it though: If we take stock of our failures, there is no end to what we learn. The determined leader will not be denied ultimate success.

Behold the Victory

The place to begin is with the end—with the vision of the completed church in the consummation of all things. Jesus has promised that the church He is building shall be finished (Matt. 16:13–18; Mark 8:27–30; Luke 9:18–20). Despite the assault of treacherous principalities of evil, His church will emerge victorious, not merely surviving the assaults, but taking the offensive, gaining mastery over the enemy, until every foe is defeated. Nothing can ultimately prevail against world evangelization. However fierce the battle in this present age, His church is triumphant.

This victory rings through the Gospel of the Kingdom. Jesus is Lord! He has conquered sin and death; the gates of hell have been torn down. The crucified and risen Messiah-King saves unto the uttermost everyone who comes unto God through Him. In glory and majesty He now reigns upon the throne of heaven, from whence He will return in glory to judge the nations in righteousness and truth.

Any compromise regarding the historical finality of Christ's life and mission destroys the Gospel at its source. That is why theological liberalism inevitably decimates evangelism and brings church decline. It has no reproductive vitality, for it has no life-giving Gospel.

We reproduce what we believe.[1] If we believe that Christ is no more than a great moral teacher who only offers the best of many religious options, then we will politely ignore the exclusive demands of His Kingdom. But if we truly believe that Jesus Christ is the Lord of heaven and earth and that His finished work at Calvary alone

---

1. Probably the best comprehensive treatment of this thesis, both its theological basis and methodological practice, is the reference volume of the addresses and papers presented at the International Congress on World Evangelization in Lausanne, Switzerland, in 1974, J. D. Douglas, ed., *Let the Earth Hear His Voice* (Minneapolis, Minn.: World Wide Pubs., 1975). The two-volume collection of papers and reports of the earlier World Congress on Evangelism, in Berlin, in 1966, also is excellent. Carl F. H. Henry and W. Stanley Mooneyham, eds., *One Race, One Gospel, One Task* (Minneapolis, Minn.: World Wide Pubs., 1967). A more specialized collection, but equally relevant, is the volume of addresses at the International Congress for Itinerant Evangelists in Amsterdam in 1983, J. D. Douglas, ed., *The Work of an Evangelist* (Minneapolis, Minn.: World Wide Pubs., 1984).

brings salvation to a lost world, then we will go forth to herald His Name to every creature.[2] Whatever the creed espoused, disciples of Christ who do not express this concern simply do not take their faith seriously.

Too quickly is this issue passed over in church growth discussions, even within the evangelical community. Much of what is said on this subject comes largely from sociological and behavioristic research, not the content of the Christian mission. The result is that interest turns primarily to humanistic considerations, like more astute communication techniques or better institutional programs. All this is helpful, of course, but unless there is genuine commitment to the essential Gospel of Christ, merely changing ways of doing things is like rearranging chairs on the *Titanic*. We must come to grips with the faith once delivered to the saints and then let it set our agenda.

Girded by the apostles' doctrine, we will be constrained to think big. Why not? Nothing is too hard for God.

---

2. In an extensively documented study of nearly 300 pages, entitled *The Evangelization of the Roman Empire* (Macon, Ga.: Mercer Univ. Press, 1981), E. Glenn Hinson concluded that the spread of the church during the first few centuries was related "to an exclusivism and intolerance" inculcated through their "ecclesiastical and theological forms." This to him meant that "early Christianity grew for the basic reasons that conservative American churches are now growing." Then, after disclaiming any personal support of his own findings, he added that it is "doubtful whether many modern Christians would look with favor on the disciplinary procedures or on the authoritarian ministry of the early centuries." At this point he confided that the Christian faith should not see itself "so much in competition with other world religions as in cooperation or in conjunction with them" (287). The astounding thing about his position is not its universalistic bent, but that he takes it in open contradiction to a principle he knows is true, which admittedly still pertains to growing churches.

Every church needs to view its commitment from the standpoint of the coming Kingdom. Only in the light of eternity dare we plan for the present.

It would be well for us, individually and as a church, to set some realistic goals to help keep the vision before us. They could include spiritual objectives in terms of character formation as well as growth in church membership and ministries. In view of our resources, where do we believe God wants us to be five, ten, twenty, years hence? General objectives might be broken down into more specialized categories, such as increase of disciples, our prayer life, involvement in missions, giving, and the like. As statements of faith, the goals should be specific as to nature, attainable in reference to time, and measurable by an objective means of evaluation.[3] Priorities can then be determined on the basis of these aspirations and strategies developed to meet them.

Concentrate on Learners

While envisioning the victory of the church to the ends of the earth, we should avoid unrealistic projections. There is nothing in the apostolic experience to suggest

---

3. Much has been written about goal setting in recent years. For an introduction to this practice, see Dale D. McConkey, *Goal Setting: A Guide to Achieving the Church's Mission* (Minneapolis, Minn.: Augsburg Press, 1978); or Daniel L. Mead and Darrel J. Allen, *Ministry by Objectives* (Wheaton, Ill.: Evangelical Teacher Training Assoc., 1978). If it is felt that more expertise is needed in church planning with goals in mind, the book by Edward R. Dayton and Ted W. Engstrom will be helpful, *Strategy for Leadership* (Old Tappan, N.J.: Fleming H. Revell, 1979). A concise bibliography lists other resources.

that vast populations are going to quickly embrace the Gospel. People are largely disposed to materialistic interests, and even their religious inclinations tend to be self-serving. Good-natured though they may be, the multitudes are too preoccupied with their own pleasure to go against the tide of worldliness about them. Compounding the problem, those in privileged positions of leadership, who should inspire nobler desires, most often are themselves drifting along the downward path of least resistance.

Realistically, then, before much can be done to lift the vision of the masses, something must be done to multiply the authentic witness of Christians close to them. It follows that whatever form our evangelism takes, winning and training disciples to disciple others must have preeminence. The aimless multitudes of the world must have a leader to follow who knows the way of Christ: someone they trust, who can show them the meaning of the Kingdom. Merely telling people what to believe will not suffice. They must see the Gospel incarnated consistently in the lives of their friends.

Such people do not come by accident. They are raised up by God in answer to prayer. As we look to Him in faith, we can be assured that He will draw those to us whom we can disciple. They will be recognized by their yearning to learn more of the Savior. Probably those attracted by our love will already have some natural ties with us, such as race, culture, age, sex, hobbies, education, or vocation. So building a friendship will not be difficult. Whether or not they occupy a prominent position of leadership makes no difference, for in their own sphere of influence, just as in our own, there will be ample opportunity to disciple.

On a larger scale, the selection principle applies to the community evangelistic thrust of a congregation. As with each of us individually, the church should concentrate evangelistic efforts upon persons most open to the Gospel. Not that others are ignored, but that our resources are limited and the receptivity of people helps determine where investment will bring the greatest returns for the Kingdom. Understanding what people are thinking also assists in devising methods most effective in reaching them.[4]

Let me note, however, that determinations of priority should not be advertised, least of all in discipling. In fact, the less said publicly about it, the better. A wise general does not tell his battle plans to the troops. There will be time enough to share details of the strategy when our disciples have matured in their leadership.

Stay Together

The way these aspiring leaders will develop is through association. If they are to learn the meaning of the Christ life, we must be together enough for them to see it lived out. This is the essence of the plan followed by Jesus with His disciples and continued in His church. The principle was woven into their whole structure of corporate meetings for fellowship, teaching, and worship as well as their system of on-the-job training. Truth was not taught in abstract doctrines or regulations; it was caught in the experience of their shared life.

---

4. The level of receptivity within a group will influence the manner in which the Gospel is presented. How this can be determined is discussed by James F. Engel, *How Can I Get Them to Listen?* (Grand Rapids, Mich.: Zondervan, 1977); and by the same author in collaboration with W. Wilbert Norton, *What's Gone Wrong with the Harvest?* (Grand Rapids, Mich.: Zondervan, 1975).

This is the way we learn in the family. All the early church did was relate their faith to this most elemental law of learning. In so doing they facilitated education, while also expressing their solidarity. No one could feel isolated. An environment was created for realistic follow-up and discipleship, whereby the body of believers ministered to one another, both individually and collectively.

The same atmosphere for learning is needed today. Church meetings and activities, whatever their nature, must provide a setting for camaraderie in the bonds of Christ. It is not a matter of stressing unstructured gatherings at the expense of formal services. The apostolic community would teach us that both spontaneity and formality, freedom and structure, serve the body purpose, when love comes through.[5]

This sense of belonging is especially crucial with new converts. To make sure that it is not missed, particularly on the personal level, every beginning pilgrim needs one or two Christian friends close by, to constantly encourage growth. The relationship is best developed when relaxed and unpretentious, like eating meals or doing things together. In the process they will observe the values and disciplines that mold our lives. Though to others these casual meetings may appear quite spontaneous, they usually have to be carefully planned. A church can assist the effort by arranging for qualified sponsors to get with beginning saints on a continuing basis until such time as

---

5. In a study of thirty-eight denominations by the Institute for American Church Growth, a direct relationship was found between the percentage of "people feeling loved" and the growth of that denomination. *Executive Growth Report*, vol. 10 (1986), 2.

the new disciples are spiritually strong enough to reproduce.[6]

One way to facilitate more authentic sharing, for the
new Christians as well as the old, is through the multiplication of small groups within the church constituency.
The size of the congregation makes no difference.[7] These
groups might take form around any number of interests—Bible study, Sunday school, prayer, missionary society, choir, special ministries, ladies' tea, men's
breakfast, youth, hobbies, senior-citizen activities, deacons' board, professional occupations, neighborhood
friendships—almost any focus of commonality that can
bring together like-minded people in the Name of Christ.
The groups can determine their own procedures and discipline, but whatever the design, each person in the fel-

6. Programs of this kind are generally available through the
church. Consult your denominational headquarters if help is needed.
Also, excellent resources are available from a number of service or-
ganizations, such as the Navigators, Campus Crusade for Christ,
Churches Alive, International Evangelism Association and World
Wide Discipleship Association. On the personal level of follow-up
and discipleship, there is no want of information from disciplers who
have written in this area, including Dawson Trotman, Keith Phillips,
Bill Hull, Carl Wilson, Charles Shaver, Frances Cosgrove, Waylon
Moore, John MacArthur, Allen Hadidian, Gary W. Kuhne, Doug
Hartman, Gene Warr, Walter A. Henrichsen, William A. Shell, Dan
Crawford, Donald Jenson, William Peterson, Juan Carlos Ortiz,
among many others. A brief bibliography of written sources will be
found in Billie Hanks, Jr., *Discipleship: The Best Writings from the
Most Experienced Disciple Makers* (Grand Rapids, Mich.: Zonder-
van, 1981), 189, 190.

7. The Seoul Gospel Central Church, the world's largest congregation, with 500,000 members, fosters more than 30,000 small
groups, meeting mostly in homes. For an explanation of the way
these groups function, see the pastor's account, Paul Yong-gi Cho,
Successful Home Cell Groups (Plainfield, N.J.: Logos Intl., 1981).

lowship should seek for every other member the highest in God's purpose. Such relationships grow loving leaders in the church family.[8]

Mobilize for Ministry

Fellowship, however, is not an end in itself. The times together serve to prepare the church for her mission in the world. Unless expression is given to the servant role of the body, the redeemed community becomes a contradiction to the mission that gave her birth and eventually dries up in self-adulation. I suspect that this danger is far more real than we like to admit. Just ask the hurting people who live around the church neighborhood.

It is our business to find the needs of these folk and seek to meet them. We dare not sit idly by and expect them to come to us. A shepherd goes after the lost sheep. Likely those things brought first to our attention will be on the temporal level, where the anxieties of the masses usually center. This calls for a relevant response. Local churches can stimulate involvement by offering meaning-

---

8. Information about the mission and operation of small groups is easily obtainable. If one needs help in getting started, some of the introductions include William Clemmons and Harvey Hester, *Growth Through Groups* (Nashville, Tenn.: Broadman Press, 1974); Richard Peace, *Small Group Evangelism* (Downers Grove, Ill.: Inter-Varsity, 1985); Lawrence O. Richards, *A New Face for the Church* (Grand Rapids, Mich.: Zondervan, 1970); and a Navigator Guide, *How to Lead Small Group Bible Studies* (Colorado Springs, Colo.: NavPress, 1985). For many creative group exercises, *see* Lyman Coleman's *Encyclopedia of Serendipity* (Littleton, Colo.: Serendipity House, 1980); and by the same author, the *Mastering the Basics* Bible study, an excellent integrated program for self and group study, combined with expository teaching.

ful social programs for the community, utilizing the various gifts of the saints, while also drawing upon the provisions of divine grace. We need not be intimidated by the limitations of our natural resources, for in God's will, there is always the possibility of supernatural intervention in healing and deliverance. Ministering to the whole person, of course, uncovers the necessity for a saving Gospel. Apart from this spiritual reference, our work would still leave people without ultimate hope. So woven through the concern for the physical and emotional welfare of people must be a caring ministry to their souls. Evangelism finally becomes the most essential expression of our love.

Everyone in the church can do something. How the people accept this principle and exercise their priesthood will largely determine the impact of their witness upon society. Some specially called members, like the pastor-teacher, have a unique responsibility in equipping believers for the task, but they are not expected to carry the whole load. All of us have gifts and skills through which the Great Commission can be fulfilled.[9] When it is seen as a life-style, then even secular occupations take on the meaning of the sacred, and every activity can become a means of making disciples.

The greatest opportunity for ministry comes in day-by-day witnessing in the home and at work, where personal

---

9. Representative of the rather voluminous literature on spiritual gifts are the books by Kenneth O. Gargel, *Unwrap Your Spiritual Gifts* (Wheaton, Ill.: Victor Books, 1983); Mary R. Schramm, *Gifts of Grace* (Minneapolis, Mich.: Augsburg Press, 1982); and C. Peter Wagner, *Your Spiritual Gifts Can Help Your Church Grow* (Ventura, Calif.: Regal, 1979).

relationships are virtually automatic.[10] Also, there are any number of church programs that need personnel, not the least being the follow-up of new Christians. As disciples develop in self-confidence and proficiency, more difficult work assignments can be delegated, such as leading a Bible class, directing a visitation campaign, or serving on an important committee. Eventually, mature workers move into major positions of leadership, perhaps assuming the office of deacon or elder.

By the time these persons take leading roles in the church, they should themselves be deeply involved in discipling a few persons, thus giving the larger body an example to follow. As their disciples in turn become disciplers, the mobilization of the potential work force accelerates, assuring an ever-expanding ministry to the world.

The church can assist this outreach by providing structures through which believers can function as a body.[11]

---

10. Written resources in methods of personal evangelism are readily available. However, before getting submerged in research, let me suggest to anyone wanting help to ask a Christian more proficient in this area to let you go along in some witnessing experiences. An illustration will be worth more than any book you can read. If there is time to do some reading, find an author who speaks your language and seems to make sense. Among the hundreds who have addressed this subject are W. Oscar Thompson, Jr., Joseph C. Aldrich, Billie Hanks, Jr., Charles Kingsley, James Kennedy, Leighton Ford, Mark McCloskey, Stephen Olford, Matthew Prince, Stanley Tam, Bill Bright, Leroy Eims, Jard DeVille, Jonathan Gainsbrugh, Howard Hendricks, Arthur G. McPhee, Paul Little, Rebecca Manley Pippert, Jim Peterson, John White, to mention only a few. A good selected bibliography can be found in G. William Schweer, *Personal Evangelism for Today* (Nashville, Tenn.: Broadman Press, 1984), 187–192.

11. Programs for local church evangelism are as numerous as they are different. Follow the method best suited to your situation. If you

One effective approach will be the organization of teams to work together in specially targeted places of need. Often these groups can become the nucleus for planting a new congregation, thereby establishing another center of outreach, starting the cycle of growth again.

Church planting, however, like any other extension program, will not produce the desired results unless those who do the work are themselves disciplers. Organizational activities cannot rise above the level of their leaders. Would it not then be appropriate to ask, "Are those

do not know how a congregation can be organized around this purpose, check with your denominational evangelism department, or better still, consult with the staff of a church that is evangelistically effective. Such a congregation will not be hard to locate, for probably it is the fastest growing, most vibrant church in town. Among persons who have written in this field are Frank R. Tillapough, Lewis A. Drummond, David Watson, Chuck Smith, C. B. Hogue, Ralph Neighbor, Jerry Falwell, Jerry Cook, Charles Shumate, Samuel Shoemaker, Jack Hayford, George Sweazy, Samuel Southard, Paul Benjamin, Mendall Taylor, Roy Fish, Robert Schuller, J. E. Conant, Jerry Kirk, Oscar I. Romo, George G. Hunter III, Win Arn, Howard Ball, Paul Cedar, Lyle Shaller, and Sterling W. Huston. For practical help in this area by a wide variety of church leaders, see the four-volume reproducible notebook containing the thoughts of approximately 200 spokesmen at the American Festival of Evangelism in Kansas City in 1981 (P.O. Box 17093, Washington, D.C. 20041). Another series with a representative group of evangelism leaders, both Protestant and Roman Catholic, is edited by Glenn C. Smith in four volumes, the first being *Evangelizing Adults,* jointly published by Tyndale House in Wheaton and the Paulist National Catholic Evangelization Assoc., Washington, D.C., 1985. The vast church-growth literature also offers much insight. How this movement has developed and its basic approach are discussed by Delos Miles, *Church Growth—A Mighty River* (Nashville, Tenn.: Broadman, 1981). To get a comprehensive view of various models of church growth today, check Elmer Towns, John Vaughan, and David J. Seifert *The Complete Book of Church Growth,* 2nd ed. (Wheaton, Ill.: Tyndale, 1985). A bibliography is appended.

few persons close to us seeing the life-style of our Lord? Will they be able to impart it to others?"

Live Under Orders

What they do will tell the story. However correct may be our teaching, unless the learners follow the truth, it avails nothing. So in making disciples, beginning with conversion and extending throughout life, obedience must be understood as the outworking of faith. Not only does it make believers available for service, but it assures that there will be no foreclosure on progress. Apart from faithfulness, the training process would end.

It follows that reasonable expectations of obedience must be accepted by the church. I am not thinking of membership vows—commitments that the adherents have already taken—but the practical way in which our affirmations are implemented in life. What this means may need to be spelled out in some minimum disciplines, like personal devotional habits of prayer and Bible reading, stewardship of time and resources, community concern, including a ministry requirement.[12] The obligations are not intended as a legalistic code, but guidelines by which advancement can be encouraged.

Once accepted, a system should be devised to make ourselves accountable. Personal discipling relationships, reinforced by meetings of the church, provide the necessary structure. Without prying, yet with firmness, we need

---

12. An example of a training program with this focus is "A Disciple's Bifocals," designed to enlarge the world vision of a local church, available through the Association of Church Missions Committees, P.O. Box ACMC, Wheaton, IL 60189.

to inquire about the welfare of one another. What about our prayer life? How are things at home? Have we been diligent in bearing witness to our faith? Attitudes come in for review as well as actions. Where negligence is discovered, rebuke may be necessary in love.[13] At the same time, we should freely commend good traits and affirm the gifts and self-worth of persons with us.

Half-hearted, lukewarm commitment can never be condoned in the ranks of God's army. We are engaged in mortal combat with all the principalities of darkness, and the battle will grow more intense as the end of the age approaches. Nothing less than total allegiance to our Commander-in-chief qualifies soldiers for battle. Christ's call is to martyrdom—to die to our own self-appointed ways, in loving submission to the will of God. His Word is our command, His cross the measure of our obedience. Such consecration may be looked upon as fanaticism by the worldly-wise, but it is the stuff the New Testament church is made of: daring faith that does not think of limits or make excuses; a willingness to go wherever Christ leads, never to stop until His work is finished and the commendation is heard, "Well done thou good and faithful servant."

Receive the Power

The Holy Spirit puts it all together. What God administers as the Father and reveals as the Son, He accom-

---

13. A helpful treatment of this subject is by John White and Ken Blue, *Healing the Wounded* (Downers Grove, Ill.: InterVarsity Press, 1985). It is discussed from the standpoint of the congregation by J. Carl Leney, *A Guide to Church Discipline* (Minneapolis, Minn.: Bethany House, 1985).

plishes as the Third Member of the Trinity. So the mission of Christ through His church becomes the acts of the Spirit. He lifts up the Word, and as Jesus is glorified men and women are drawn unto the Father. Here is the secret of the Great Commission. It is finally God's work, not ours. We are merely the channel through which the Spirit of Christ makes disciples.

He it is who gives the vision of the Kingdom and enables us to project plans to reach our world with the Gospel. The Spirit draws out disciples, planting in their hearts the desire to learn; our part is to respond to His initiative. He forms the body of believers, giving unity and love to the fellowship. The indwelling Counselor calls the church to ministry and dispenses gifts for service. Through His strength faith comes alive in obedience, and by His impartation of grace, we are conformed to the character of our Lord.

Everything, then, depends upon the Spirit's possession of the sent ones, the church. Just as those first disciples were told to tarry until they received the promised power, so must we. The spiritual enduement of Pentecost, by whatever name it is called, must be a reality in our lives, not as a distant memory, but as a present experience of the reigning Christ.[14] Hindrances that obstruct His dominion need to be confessed, and our hearts need to be cleansed so that the Spirit of holiness can fill us with the love of God. Though we can never contain all of Him, He

---

14. Some helpful readings pertaining to the Spirit's fullness are noted in Robert E. Coleman, *The Master Plan of Evangelism* (Old Tappan, N.J.: Fleming H. Revell, 1964), 69, 70. An appeal for sensitivity when considering this promise of grace, whatever our particular doctrinal point of view, is by George Mallone, *Furnace of Renewal* (Downers Grove, Ill.: InterVarsity Press, 1981), 163–179.

wants all of us—to love Him and adore Him with all that we are and all that we hope to be.

This is the challenge before the church of the Great Commission. How we respond will largely determine the impact of our witness upon eternity. While the ultimate dimensions of the coming Kingdom are not yet visible, we know that when the Son of Man appears, then we shall be like Him, for we shall see Him as He is, and every knee shall bow before Him and every tongue declare to the glory of the Father that Jesus Christ is Lord.